# Wild & Free in the City

To Annie,

Your unwavering love and the way you've shown me the beauty of being in nature have been my guiding light throughout this journey. In your presence, I've rediscovered the profound connection we share with the natural world. This book is a tribute to the inspiration you've breathed into my life and a reminder that our bond with nature is at the heart of our existence.

# Wild & Free in the City

An Urbanite's Guide to Finding Nature's Pulse
Amid the Hustle

ISBN: 978-1-304-96111-2

For information, contact: rodney@coachrodneyking.com

Printed in the United States of America.

Visit: www.naturelead.earth

Table of Contents

# Foreword

I had the pleasure of supervising Rodney during his recent masters research on nature guides. I was impressed by his intelligence, deep insight and experience as a nature-based practitioner. His compassion and love for the natural world that we all belong to was abundantly clear, and this, alongside his academic study, has made Rodney into an ideal expert in the field. Most of all though, I was astounded by how in tune with nature he is, and his deep-rooted connection with all life.

This deep, personal connection with nature is one that Rodney is passionate about sharing so it is no surprise that this book takes you on a lived journey of reconnection, through Rodney's own personal and profound insights. By blending academic, practitioner and personal perspectives, it takes you through not only the background to, and malaise experienced by humanity due to our current relationship with the rest of nature, but also succinctly expresses the practical ways in which we can find a lost part of ourselves through reconnection.

This makes the book an indispensable guide to how people can practically reconnect with nature. I'll certainly be recommending it to all my students and any professionals interested in Nature Connectedness for the wonderful starting point on the area it provides and hopefully the inspiration for their (and your own) journey of reconnection with the more than human world to which we all belong.

**Dr Ryan Lumber**
Charted psychologist, creator of the Pathways Framework and expert on Nature-Connectedness

# Introduction

We are the children of the stars and the earth. Our species, Homo Sapiens, was born in the heart of nature, under the vast open sky, surrounded by the whispering trees, the singing birds, the running rivers, and the beating heart of the wild. For millennia, we roamed the vast expanses of land, guided by the rising sun and the northern star. Our bodies and minds developed in symbiosis with nature's ebb and flow, living a life inseparably woven into the fabric of the planet that gave us birth.

But as time passed, we paved over the green with grey, replacing forests with skyscrapers and rivers with roads. We created dazzlingly complex and vibrant cities, marvels of human creativity and technological prowess, encapsulating our dreams, ambitions, and triumphs. These cities have offered us unprecedented convenience, prosperity, and knowledge, but at a cost that we are only just beginning to understand.

In our pursuit of progress and in the name of convenience, we've isolated ourselves from the symphony of the natural world that we evolved to be a part of. We've wrapped ourselves in walls of concrete and screens of light, increasingly disconnected from the wind on our skin, the soil beneath our feet, and the chorus of life that once sang us to sleep.

"Wild & Free in the City" is a beacon for those who yearn for the lost connection, a guide for the city-dweller whose soul longs for the green and the wild amidst the urban jungle. It aims to illustrate the deeply-rooted ties between our well-being and our relationship with nature, ties that have been overlooked and under-appreciated in the hustle of modern life.

Our journey through the pages of this book will reveal that the wilderness is not a distant, inaccessible realm but is available within our reach, within the city's heart, and within our souls. We will explore dozens of accessible, practical ways to reintroduce nature into our daily lives, not as an idyllic, distant dream, but as a tangible, everyday reality.

The practices and rituals outlined here are not only about observing, but also about participating, immersing ourselves back into nature's rhythm. They will invite you to feel the rain, to witness the change of seasons, to recognise the wildlife thriving in our cities, and even to grow your own green sanctuaries.

As we chart this journey together, you'll discover that being 'wild and free' is not just about venturing into the great outdoors but a state of mind, a conscious choice to live harmoniously with the Earth's rhythm, even in a city. It is about nurturing our mental health, resilience, and well-being through a profound connection with the natural world that has the power to heal, invigorate, and inspire us.

It is time for us to remember what it means to be truly human. To recognise that we are not separate entities living on the Earth, but an integral part of the Earth living. It's time to bring the wild back into our hearts, to set free the nature-loving spirit within us, even amidst the bustling cityscapes. Because no matter where we build our homes, the song of the wild is within us, ready to sing again.

Welcome to "Wild & Free in the City". May your journey be filled with discovery, healing, and a renewed connection to the world that waits outside your door and inside your heart.

# Shaping Inspiration from Psychedelic Spores: The Genesis of this Book

"Wild & Free in the City" - my literary love letter to our planet - sprouted from a profound, transformative odyssey undertaken in the company of two close friends and mushrooms. My voyage into the realm of psilocybin, a potent psychedelic, served as a beacon guiding me to a deeper understanding of the universe and the spiritual perspectives woven into its intricate tapestry.

The universe unfurled itself to me, not as a chaotic confluence of random atoms and particles but as an effervescent, continually evolving entity pulsating with sentient intelligence. It is an entity that compels conscious life forms to become vessels for its vast wisdom. This revelatory understanding, gifted by the mushrooms, enlightened me to the universal interconnectivity of all beings, casting a luminous glow on the inherent elegance and complexity of existence.

The Andean concept of 'Pachamama' - a wisdom passed down from the indigenous people of South America - vividly encapsulates this understanding. When translated, it signifies 'Mother Earth' or 'Mother Universe', echoing a profound belief in the sentient, living nature of our world, woven into the fabric of every life form.

The mushrooms revealed to me a universe bound by

an unseen lattice where each action, every thought, sends ripples through the cosmos, affecting the whole. I felt the warm embrace of this cosmic web, awakening to the immense impact of my thoughts and actions on the universe's pulse. This realisation catalysed my commitment to infusing positivity into my environment.

The indigenous concept of 'Mitakuye Oyasin' from the Lakota Sioux of North America, mirrors this universal interconnectedness. It signifies 'all my relations', underscoring the profound realisation that we are all tethered together in the cosmic dance.

My journey also illuminated the enduring nature of our bonds with loved ones, transcending the physical realm's confines. I discerned that our connections are not shackled by time or space but echo in the heartbeats of our souls. This understanding aligns with the Quechua concept from South America, 'Unsihuay', translating to 'the power of the heart'. It attests to the sustenance and fortification of our relationships through the enduring qualities of love and compassion.

Amid this mystical pilgrimage, my communion with Gaia, the living embodiment of our planet, deepened. Through the fungal conduit, Gaia voiced her suffering and pleaded for my empathy. I vividly remember a tear-streaked night under the cosmos when she made me feel her agony—the earth beneath me seeming to burn with her pain. Yet, she whispered reassurances: "I'll endure, but I need your assistance." This stark revelation exposed our planet's fragility and beckoned me to safeguard it for the generations to come.

The Lakota Sioux sentiment of 'Ina Maka', translating to 'Mother Earth' or 'Earth Mother', embodies this call. It emphasises our duty to protect and respect the living, breathing entity that is our world.

This psychedelic journey underscored the privilege of inhabiting this planet and reinforced my belief that there's no better moment than the present, no place more significant than here. Gaia has entrusted me with a message—calling for a global shift toward positive change. It's a message I believe needs a global audience, a collective embrace, and proactive implementation—for our well-being and the survival of our planet.

Without this transcendent journey, I doubt "Wild & Free in the City" would have found its way onto the page. The book is an ode to Mother Nature's plea for help, a beacon amid the stormy seas of environmental uncertainty.

For a time, I was burdened by the question, "How can I assist?"

The global challenges we face seem monumental, overwhelming. Our beautiful Gaia is in distress, slowly suffocating under the weight of our actions. As an avid globetrotter, I've borne witness to the devastating impacts of human activity on our natural world. One glaring example is from a recent trip to Thailand. Walking along the litter-strewn beaches, my partner and I were stricken by the pervasive degradation - a sight that moved her to tears repeatedly.

Yet, the question persisted, "What can I do to help?"

I'm not a policymaker or a world leader, just a single man awakened to the terrifying reality that if we continue on our current trajectory, we risk bequeathing a barren world to future generations.

This book is my modest attempt to shed light on our disconnection from the natural world. It doesn't claim to have all the answers but seeks to unravel the historical threads that led us to estrangement from our true home—Gaia. I aim to explore ways we, as urban dwellers in the modern world, can reconnect with nature in our concrete jungles. I firmly believe in shifting our global consciousness from a paradigm of scarcity, competition, and fear to one resonating with spirit, harmony, respect, responsibility, and wisdom.

In the spirit of this transition, I aspire to ignite a spark of connectivity in my readers, prompting them to begin rekindling their bond with nature, even within the heart of the urban jungle. I strongly believe that one solution to our declining mental health in the modern world is to unearth ways to reconnect with nature.

Reconnecting to nature isn't a panacea for all modern-day afflictions; it is, however, a potent antidote to the ceaseless onslaught of anxiety-inducing speed and overwhelm we encounter daily in our modern landscapes. My hope is that this book assists you in reclaiming your innate wild health. As you reconnect to nature, I hope it fosters in you a deep reverence and respect for our natural world. If more of us can learn to value the vibrancy of nature, even in our city parks, we will start to care deeply for all of nature. It's not just about our survival as a species, but also our role as custodians of this planet. This, I believe, is our true purpose—our call to action.

*I have always been fascinated by mushrooms of all kinds. I took this photo of the classic fairy tale toadstool, the Fly agaric. This red and white fungus is often found beneath birch trees on the Isle of Man during autumn.*

# A Return to Wild Health

Though my journey to inspiration originated in an enlightening communion with mushrooms, the expedition to reclaim my wild health was not without its significant trials. My upbringing, mired in the deprivation of government housing on Johannesburg's South Side, instilled in me a primal instinct for survival. My days were defined not only by evading the lurking dangers of our treacherous streets but also by steeling myself for the inevitable tempest of home, where an abusive, alcohol-addicted mother held court. Years of physical and psychological torment unfolded, culminating in a night when, fuelled by intoxication, she cast me out. I was seventeen, homeless, and left to navigate the ruthless labyrinth of Johannesburg's inner city.

Confronted by this harsh reality, I sought refuge in the military before I had even marked my 18th year, during an era when conscription was a mandatory rite of passage in South Africa. Once I'd parted ways with the military, devoid of formal education or clear prospects, I dedicated myself to ceaseless labour. By my early thirties, I had seemingly amassed the societal trophies of success—a luxury sports car, a desirable home, a flourishing career as a martial arts coach, and an academic resume boasting numerous accolades. Yet, beneath the veneer of these accomplishments, a profound dissatisfaction lurked.

My discontent was compounded by a stark revelation from my neurologist: the years of arduous physical training had waged a silent war on my body. My neck was degenerating, and recurrent blows to the head had started to gnaw at my well-being. Paired with a sting of betrayal in my business ventures, I descended into a debilitating bout of depression.

The year 2019 heralded a painful divorce and an accompanying yearning for renewal. Serendipity guided me towards the idyllic Isle of Man, synchronistically coinciding with the advent of Covid-enforced lockdowns. The imposed limitations of movement and activity nudged me towards the comfort of the natural world. My days became a meditative exploration of verdant meadows and forests, with my footprints etching trails along the coastal fringe. Over the course of the lockdown, my health and spirit gradually recovered. In the tranquillity of the Isle of Man, I found echoes of my childhood's fleeting moments of joy spent on my aunt's humble farm in the African bush.

This transformation was so profound that it ignited in me a desire to delve deeper into nature's therapeutic capacities. Subsequently, I qualified as a nature-based therapist and embarked on a second master's degree, focusing on the pivotal role of nature-based therapists in achieving therapeutic objectives for their clients.

My turbulent upbringing disconnected me from nature, as survival took precedence. The relentless pursuit of societal markers of success further distanced me from the rhythms of the natural world. However, I was able to excavate and reclaim my innate wildness and freedom. It is my fervent hope that this book will inspire you to unearth your own wild nature and to seek solace, healing, and rebirth in the nurturing embrace of Mother Earth.

*Perched on a cliff off Marine Drive, overlooking Port Soderick on the Isle of Man, is a spot with magnificent views over the bay. When I first arrived on the island, this was one of the first places I retreated to in my journey back to wild health.*

# Embarking on the Journey to Unleash our Wild & Free Selves

I am acutely aware that this book sometimes relies on references and scientific evidence to support concepts that, in a bygone era, would have been self-evident. Take, for instance, the extensive research validating the mental health advantages of spending time in nature. If you were to share this insight with an indigenous individual, they might respond with a puzzled look. To them, the notion that nature is beneficial for our well-being is an unquestionable truth, devoid of the need for scientific validation.

This reality underscores just how far we have strayed from our instinctive comprehension of what truly nourishes us in today's modern world. It seems we now need guidance on how to live meaningful lives. We are surrounded by an array of psychological strategies and therapies, each purporting to be the panacea for our mental health issues. One example is our reliance on research to justify and promote beneficial practices such as mindfulness. In addition, the proliferation of self-help literature attests to our diminishing trust in our innate ability to flourish independently and the subsequent need for external direction towards achieving tranquillity and balance. And yet, we remain fragmented into opposing factions, entrenched in disputes primarily fuelled by ego, offering little respite from our collective desolation.

Speak to most people today, and it's likely they'll confess that despite its pledges of affluence and joy, the modern world often leaves them feeling inexplicably enraged, anxious, lonely, and fearful, aching for a sense of purpose. Despite this, we persist in subscribing to the prevailing worldview, stubbornly hoping that our existential unrest will dissipate if we invest just a little more trust in the system. Few are prepared to confront the uncomfortable reality that our societal epidemic of emotional and spiritual turmoil can be traced back to our prevailing modern worldview—a worldview constructed on an unnatural way of existence.

While it's vital to avoid romanticising the past, it's clear that we emerged as entities profoundly intertwined with the natural world. This is our 'nest', our sanctuary. Our origin story doesn't revolve around skyscrapers and pollution. Of all conceivable environments, we came into existence as part of nature, woven into Earth's diverse tapestry of life. Our relationship with nature is indelible; we breathe the same air our ancestors did millions of years ago and consume food cultivated in soils fertile for millennia. Our forebears faced substantial challenges living off the land, but they didn't merely survive—they flourished.

A close Inspection of our terrestrial ancestors suggests that, in spite of their adversities, they possibly experienced more joy than many of us in today's modern world. While I will provide research to support this, I am convinced that we don't need validation to accept that our most rewarding and fulfilling moments transpire when we're deeply connected with our 'nest', our sanctuary, Mother Earth. My aspiration for this book is to awaken your inherent wildness and rekindle ancient memories of why re-establishing this connection with Earth is vital, not only for your personal well-being but also for the welfare of society as a whole.

Although I, like you, may not possess the capacity to significantly shift the modern societal worldview, I am committed to instigating change one individual at a time. If we all begin to accept and act upon the understanding that returning to our natural state enhances our mental health and overall well-being, we could potentially influence societal attitudes towards a more favourable direction.

So, let us embark on this journey!

# The Resilience Found in the Wild and Free

In the frantic rhythm of our modern lives, punctuated by harsh concrete landscapes, an onslaught of digital distractions, and the baffling dynamics of socio-political realities, we find ourselves yearning for the comforting echo from the past: "All good things are wild and free"[1]. This stirring sentiment by Thoreau reverberates throughout this book, serving as an urgent call to arms, a beacon for those longing to mend the growing divide between the urban multitude and the profound simplicity of nature.

Our narrative of disconnection from nature, a fairly recent addition to the human story, holds troubling implications for our shared well-being[2]. The unyielding progression of industrialisation, paired with an insatiable appetite for material wealth, has estranged us from our natural origins[3]. The Enlightenment era (1685 – 1815) disseminated the doctrine of human exceptionalism, positing that humans were above and distinct from nature[3]. This viewpoint propelled the machinery of progress, but at an expense - the cost of the inherent bond we hold with the natural world[4].

Before we chart our route back towards nature, we must first comprehend the historical shifts that led to our current disconnection. As we commence this temporal journey, remember that our exploration, while enlightening, isn't exhaustive. Still, it should impart enough understanding for us to realise that our detachment isn't an irreversible calamity but a diversion from which we can retrace our steps back to nature.

Thoreau's sage advice, a product of his profound communion with the wilderness, proposes a transformative antidote to our self-inflicted estrangement from nature. His words entreat us not to abandon our technological progress but to harmonise it with nature's rhythms. By incorporating the wisdom of our past into our present, we can sculpt a resilient future that resonates with the synergy of humans and nature.

Thoreau's philosophy is a wake-up call to humanity, encouraging us to renew our alliance with nature and acknowledge the value such a relationship bears for our collective and personal well-being. His worldview sharply diverges from the anthropocentric viewpoint of the Enlightenment and instead envisions a world where humans and nature exist in symbiosis, not hierarchy[5].

Given our current environmental challenges, Thoreau's philosophy serves as a timely nudge to re-evaluate the structures and systems that prioritise economic growth over environmental sustainability. Our rampant consumption habits and tendency to dominate nature, fuelled by capitalist ideologies, starkly contradict the harmony Thoreau envisioned[6].

We have, for an extended period, succumbed to a dominant worldview that elevates economic progress over the sustainability of the natural world[6]. Inspired by Thoreau's philosophy, we must challenge these systemic obstacles. This challenge extends beyond establishing socio-economic models that recognise our interdependence with nature. It continues into our pursuit of regaining our wild health, empowering us with the energy and resilience to not merely survive but flourish in our natural home, Gaia.

Our mission, then, is to transition from a culture of human exceptionalism and relentless growth to one where "all good things are wild and free." By doing so, we open ourselves to rekindling our relationship with nature, cultivating resilience, harmony, and balance within ourselves and our surroundings. This journey entails rediscovering or, more precisely, remembering our roles as guardians of the Earth, integral threads of the vast ecological tapestry, not its overlords.

As such, we may find ourselves at times contemplating the question, "Why are we here?"

While it may seem idealised, I argue that we are here to act as stewards of the natural world. The natural world that has nurtured us, bestowed upon us the gift of consciousness and allowed us to evolve into thoughtful beings capable of introspection, exploration, and growth.

We have not found ourselves here by accident, but by the design of the universe. To believe that we were destined to destroy our home, perhaps one of the most beautiful corners of the universe, seems contradictory to the purpose of our existence.

*One of those "why are we here?" moments.*

# The Illusion of Modernity: Unmasking Wetiko and its Paradox

As I venture deeper into the labyrinth of self-awakening, I find myself at odds with the pervasive narrative of what defines a life well-lived. A sentiment that may resonate with you, as it often rings with a discordant note of alienation, a disconnect met with baffled incredulity, if not outright dismissal, by those who adhere to the status quo.

An act of daring to question the omnipotent altar of modernity, upon which our society kneels, sends tremors through the fabric of our collective consciousness. In cultures where the tendrils of modernity have penetrated deep, such tremors are often viewed as heretical, as a blasphemy against the sacred liturgy of progress and prosperity[7]. This resistance is a testament to our entrenched indoctrination, a conditioned belief that modernity is our beacon in the storm, our pathfinder, the ultimate panacea for our existential woes.

Let's not be blind to the gifts of modernity. Our epoch has been marked by monumental achievements - scientific revolutions, medical marvels, technological wonders, and elevated standards of living[8]. For those fortunate enough to sip from the cup of modern privilege, myself included, we owe our comfort, convenience, and longevity to these triumphs of human endeavour. Yet, this narrative often omits an unsettling reality - in many corners of our world, the daily miracles we take for granted, a flick of a switch illuminating a room, the effortless flow of clean water, or a toilet's silent disposal, remain a distant mirage for millions.

However, as we stand at the precipice of the Anthropocene, it becomes vital to confront the paradox of modernity. The same forces that ushered in an era of unprecedented growth and progress are simultaneously the architects of our looming existential crises. Climate change, rampant consumption, mental health pandemics, growing income disparities, and environmental degradation are but the bitter fruits borne of modernity's insatiable quest for dominance, competition, and a materialistic paradigm [9,10].

Here, I introduce the concept of 'Wetiko', a term borrowed from Native American Algonquin tribes, encapsulating a cannibalistic spirit that ravages the host from within by engendering selfishness, greed, and myopia[11]. This metaphor serves as an unsettling mirror to the shadow side of modernity.

Wetiko syndrome presents the unsettling hypothesis that we, the denizens of the modern world, are in the throes of a collective psychological malaise. This pathology manifests in our obstinate denial or ignorance of the paradox that the very systems we champion as our saviours are also the harbingers of our own undoing[12]. Mesmerised by the gilded promises of modernity - wealth, status, power

- we turn a blind eye to the resultant afflictions on our mental health, our social fabric, and our fragile blue planet. And yet, in the grand scheme of existence, wealth, status, and power are but transient illusions, ephemeral echoes that will fade into the annals of history upon our departure.

The lingering question, then, is this: Why do we continue to endorse, propagate, and defend a system that paradoxically poisons us? The answer lies within our own cognitive dissonance, our instinctual aversion to discomfort. We opt for the comforting illusion of safety and stability, even if it means skirting the harsh reality[13]. This selective blindness is Wetiko's modus operandi, a psychological sleight of hand that keeps us oblivious to the truth.

Drawing from the wisdom of the Algonquin tribes, Wetiko symbolises a breach of sacred bonds, a violation of the symbiotic harmony within the tribe or the balance of nature[11]. When we transpose this concept onto the canvas of modernity, we discern Wetiko's footprint in the destructive, cannibalistic tendencies manifested in our socio-economic and political constructs. This contagion of selfishness and shortsightedness, as reframed in the contemporary context, feeds the relentless pursuit of profit and power at the expense of humanity and our home planet[9,10]. It fuels the engine of consumerism, where insatiable desires stoke the fires of overproduction, overconsumption, and an endless cycle of exploitation[14].

Perhaps one of the most detrimental repercussions of Wetiko Syndrome in the modern era is a deep collective amnesia, one that severs us from our true sanctuary - the natural world. This disconnection, a forced estrangement from our primal roots in nature, exacerbates the impacts of Wetiko. We have forgotten that we are not solitary entities adrift in a vacuum, but integral threads interwoven in the intricate tapestry of life. The implications of this disconnection are profound, extending into the realm of our collective mental health and well-being.

The emerging field of eco-psychology posits that the schism between humanity and nature is strongly correlated with the escalating rates of mental health disorders[15,16]. Symptoms such as isolation, anxiety, and depression could be interpreted as the visceral echoes of a deeper wound, a disconnection from the life-affirming embrace of the natural world[16]. Wetiko Syndrome, by deepening this chasm, fuels a widespread societal and individual mental health crisis.

Yet, if we heed the timeless wisdom of our indigenous ancestors, the cure for Wetiko lies within ourselves, in our ability to recognise its presence and strive towards reestablishing our lost connections with our community and the natural world. The acknowledgement of Wetiko's existence within our society and within our own psyche offers us a pathway to restore balance and heal the deep-seated wounds of disconnection. By grappling with the paradox of modernity and facing the Wetiko within us, we can start making conscious choices that align with a vision of life that is sustainable, equitable, and enriching for all.

# Reevaluating Our Collective Consciousness: Capitalism, Selfishness and The Notion of 'Survival of the Fittest'

Permeating the ether of our collective consciousness is a potent narrative that shapes our current world order. This narrative, by no means a novel observation[18], champions the unyielding hegemony of 'survival of the fittest'. It breathes life into the notion that our existence is a ceaseless battle of self-interest, a playground where capitalism, the invisible arbiter, ensures a fair and fruitful outcome.

Yet, how accurate is this lens through which we perceive our world, and how does it sculpt our societal decisions and perspectives?

The doctrine fervently propagated by this prevailing worldview is the inherent self-centeredness of humanity. Some even stretch the elasticity of this claim, employing evolutionary biology to validate their stance[19]. This belief insidiously feeds the conviction that our world is a ruthless arena where self-preservation and competition are the catalysts for progress. However, recent scientific discourse has begun to question this paradigm.

Modern research asserts that cooperative behaviour, rather than cut-throat competition, has been instrumental in the survival and evolution of numerous species, including

Homo sapiens[20]. Perhaps then, our societal prism should shift its focus from 'survival of the fittest' to 'survival of the most empathetic'.

Another bastion of this worldview is the seemingly invincible stronghold of capitalism. Many laud capitalism as the pinnacle of social and economic systems, attributing our technological miracles and improved quality of life to its reign[21]. This view, however, conveniently overlooks the glaring inequalities birthed by capitalism and the ongoing environmental catastrophe exacerbated by unregulated industrial activities[22].

Undoubtedly, capitalism has kindled significant innovation and amassed vast wealth for a privileged minority. Yet, the notion that technology, driven by market forces, will rectify all societal ills, including poverty and climate change, is a perilous oversimplification. Technological solutions often miss the systemic roots of these global challenges[23]. Moreover, the belief in perpetual economic growth is in stark conflict with our planet's finite resources[9].

The claim that humans have largely deciphered the secrets of nature, portrayed as a convoluted mechanism, uncovers another faulty belief. This anthropocentric viewpoint tends to underestimate the delicate balance of our ecosystems and the non-human entities that inhabit them[24]. In reality, our understanding of the natural world and our role within it remains shrouded in mystery. We have yet to prove ourselves as worthy custodians of Earth, given our rampant exploitation of her bounty. Yet, we boldly envision voyages beyond her borders into the cosmos. Shouldn't we strive to restore harmony with nature on our own planet before setting our sights on colonising others?

The omnipresence of the dominant worldview and its tenets in our daily exchanges, media narratives, and educational systems illustrates the profound influence of a worldview. It becomes the unacknowledged environment in which we exist, so all-pervasive that we seldom scrutinise its validity. Yet, we must remember that worldviews are not infallible truths but fabricated lenses through which we perceive reality[25]. By challenging these ubiquitous beliefs, we open the door to alternative narratives that might serve humanity and our planet more compassionately and effectively.

# A Detour from Eden: Unravelling the Historical Detachment of Western Societies from Nature

How did we get here, living in concrete jungles, so separated from our home since the dawn of mankind, the natural world?

Today, more than 4.3 billion people or 55% of the world's population, live in urban settings, and the number is expected to rise to 80% by 2050[26].

Historically, humans had a profound connection with the natural world. From hunter-gatherer societies to early agrarian communities, our ancestors relied on their intimate understanding of ecosystems and the biosphere for survival[27]. Over time, however, a complex network of societal, philosophical, technological, and economic changes has gradually pulled Western societies away from nature.

The journey of our detachment from nature dates back to the origins of agrarian society (around 10,000 BC), with the advent of the Neolithic Revolution. The shift from hunting and gathering to agriculture fundamentally transformed the relationship between humans and the environment. Instead of being an integral part of the ecosystem, humans began to manipulate and control nature to meet their needs[28].

The rise of civilisations in Mesopotamia, Egypt, and Greece saw the further distancing of humanity from nature, with urbanisation, technological advancement, and social hierarchy deepening the divide. Notably, anthropocentrism began to emerge as a philosophical tenet in Greek society. Prominent philosophers such as Aristotle and Plato posited the supremacy of human reason and intellect, implicitly placing humans above nature[29]. For instance, Plato's teacher Socrates, speaking to Phaedrus, says, "I'm a lover of learning, and trees and open country won't teach me anything, whereas men in the town do"[30]. Clearly, seeing nature as irrelevant and as non-intelligent is nothing new in the Western canon of thought.

During the Middle Ages, a critical shift occurred with the dominance of Christianity in Europe. Christianity's core narrative, as interpreted by many, established a dualistic divide between nature and humanity, with humans being endowed with a divine essence absent in nature[29]. This theological perspective laid the groundwork for the narrative of human exceptionalism that would increasingly pervade Western thought.

The Renaissance era (14th to 17th centuries) amplified this detachment, heralding a period of remarkable human-centric achievements in arts, sciences, and philosophy. Humanism, the prevailing intellectual movement, placed humans at the centre of the universe, while fostering an exploitative view of nature[31].

However, the most profound break away from nature occurred during the Enlightenment period (17th and 18th centuries). This era was marked by an unyielding belief in the power of human reason to overcome the limitations imposed by nature. Influential figures such as René Descartes and Francis Bacon advocated for the control and domination of nature through scientific exploration and technological innovation[32]. Their sentiments informed not only science but also governments and socio-economic structures, leading to an increasing detachment from nature[33].

The Industrial Revolution (late 18th to early 19th century) was a crucial turning point. The adoption of mechanised production systems fuelled by fossil fuels led to unprecedented environmental degradation and a further disconnect from nature[34]. Concurrently, the growth of capitalist economies, with their inherent emphasis on continuous expansion and resource exploitation, solidified humanity's domination over nature[35].

In the 20th and 21st centuries, urbanisation, technological progress, and economic growth have continued to drive the widening chasm between humans and nature. In the modern world, urban living, devoid of regular contact with nature, has become the norm for a significant proportion of the global population.

Clearly, the detachment of Western societies from nature has been a long and complex process driven by a multitude of interconnected societal, philosophical, technological, and economic changes. Today, as we face the unprecedented challenges of the Anthropocene, there is a pressing need to re-evaluate our relationship with the natural world and restore the balance that our ancestors once held[36].

# Human Exceptionalism: The Root of Our Disconnection

I have already mentioned the notion of human exceptionalism, but let's delve a bit deeper. The human story begins in the bosom of nature, our earliest ancestors sharing a deep and profound connection with the land, sea, and sky that nurtured them. However, as our cognitive capabilities evolved and we began to form complex societies, a transformative idea emerged: the concept of human exceptionalism[37]. This concept proposed that humans, unlike other animals, possessed unique traits and abilities that set us apart and above all other life forms. It is an idea that, as we shall see, underpins the gradual disconnection of human beings from the natural world.

Human exceptionalism is the belief that humans are fundamentally different from all other organisms on Earth, possessing certain distinctive qualities such as rationality, morality, and self-awareness[38]. This belief has been rooted in various cultures and philosophies, often attributed to divine ordination or evolutionary superiority. The traits commonly associated with human exceptionalism - such as language, tool use, self-consciousness, and moral judgment - have been seen as unique to our species, marking us out as special and superior[39].

In the Western tradition, the roots of human exceptionalism can be traced back to the Judeo-Christian heritage, where the Bible offers a vision of humans as the pinnacle of creation, given dominion over the earth and all its creatures[40]. Greek philosophers like Aristotle also bolstered these views, suggesting that humans, as rational beings, were naturally superior to animals, which were governed by mere instinct[41].

In the modern era, human exceptionalism found a solid footing in the Enlightenment, and as we saw earlier, a period marked by a faith in reason, progress, and the perfectibility of human nature[42]. Figures like Rene Descartes cemented the division between humans and animals, arguing that animals were mere machines, devoid of thought and feeling, while humans were rational beings with immortal souls[43]. Such perspectives heightened the perceived chasm between humans and nature, further consolidating the anthropocentric worldview.

This anthropocentric worldview significantly shaped societal and technological developments, leading to the detachment of humans from nature. With the advent of the industrial revolution in the late 18th and 19th centuries, this detachment was exacerbated. Powered by fossil fuels, the industrial revolution marked a shift in human civilisation from being nature-dependent to becoming nature-dominating[44]. Humans were no longer part of nature;

instead, nature was something to be harnessed, exploited, and controlled for human benefit. It is in this context that we see the emergence of capitalism as an economic system, one that thrives on the exploitation of natural resources and is essentially rooted in the ethos of human exceptionalism[35].

The belief in human exceptionalism has been instrumental in shaping our modern world. It has fostered an anthropocentric view of the world. This perspective sees humans as separate from and superior to the natural world, leading to a deep-seated alienation from nature[45]. Moreover, this belief has legitimised the exploitation of nature and the reckless pursuit of economic growth, leading to environmental degradation and an escalating ecological crisis[46].

However, the implications of human exceptionalism extend beyond environmental destruction. The estrangement from nature has profound psychological and spiritual consequences for humans. Our disconnection from nature can lead to feelings of isolation, anxiety, despair, and a sense of meaninglessness. Conversely, reconnecting with nature can have therapeutic effects, promoting mental health and well-being[47].

Furthermore, human exceptionalism also poses an epistemological challenge. By placing humans above and apart from nature, it creates a dualistic way of thinking, separating mind from body, and humans from the natural world. This separation has led to the marginalisation of intuitive, embodied, and relational ways of knowing, which were central to our ancestors' understanding of the world[48]. By contrast, modern knowledge systems, shaped by this dualistic thinking, tend to be abstract, analytical, and reductionist, often failing to grasp the holistic and interconnected nature of reality[49].

Notably, the concept of human exceptionalism is increasingly being challenged on various fronts. Ethologists and cognitive scientists have revealed striking similarities between humans and other animals in abilities such as tool use, problem-solving, empathy, and even self-awareness[50]. Meanwhile, indigenous cultures around the world offer alternative worldviews that honour the interdependence of humans and nature, challenging the anthropocentric paradigm[51].

Interestingly, in the world of quantum physics, the age-old dualities that underscore human exceptionalism—mind versus matter, observer versus observed—are being dissolved, revealing a profoundly interconnected universe where humans are no longer mere spectators but active participants[52]. In light of these developments, a re-evaluation of human exceptionalism seems not only necessary but also imminent.

Yet, despite these challenges, human exceptionalism continues to hold sway, deeply ingrained in our cultural narratives, societal structures, and individual psyches. It fuels our relentless drive for progress and expansion, often at the expense of the natural world. To shift towards a more sustainable and harmonious way of life, we must first acknowledge and question this deeply held belief.

Understanding human exceptionalism, therefore, provides a critical foundation for our journey towards reconnecting with nature and rediscovering our place in the web of life. It invites us to contemplate our true nature as human animals and challenges us to envision a world where 'humans' are no longer separate from nature but an integral part of it.

By delving into the historical roots and implications of human exceptionalism, this section sets the stage for a deep exploration of our disconnection from nature and the possibilities for reconnection. It is a journey that requires us to question our most fundamental assumptions, to embrace our vulnerability and interdependence, and to cultivate a profound sense of respect and reverence for the natural world. For, as the pioneering ecologist Aldo Leopold aptly remarked, "We abuse land because we regard it as a commodity belonging to us. When we see land as a community to which we belong, we may begin to use it with love and respect"[45].

This exploration of human exceptionalism paves the way to further delve into how this belief has shaped our present societal structures, technological advancements, and, consequently, our alienation from the natural world. This sets the stage for subsequent chapters that will explore the impacts of this disconnect and possible ways to address it, ultimately aiming to foster a healthier relationship with nature for the betterment of the human species and the planet we inhabit.

# Exploiting Nature: How Historical Paradigms Shaped Our Ecological Crisis

Earth's ongoing ecological crisis, an intricate tapestry woven over centuries, is often attributed to recent factors such as technological advancement, population growth, and consumerism. However, as we have seen at closer inspection reveals deeper threads of influence that extend back to the Enlightenment and Industrial Revolution (and arguably even further back than that). The philosophies and worldviews emanating from these eras nurtured a detached, even exploitative, vision of nature. An exploration of these historical figures' perspectives offers a profound understanding of our present environmental plight.

The Enlightenment era, as I have already noted, is often seen as the dawn of modern scientific thought. Yet, it furthered our separation from nature and amplified human domination over the natural world[53]. Francis Bacon (1561-1626), for instance, widely considered the father of modern science, advocated a dominating approach to nature. He visualised nature as a "common harlot", ripe for control and exploitation, rather than a nurturing entity[54].

This perspective was echoed by René Descartes and Thomas Hobbes, who positioned the conquest of nature as a moral obligation guided by human reason[23]. René Descartes, who was a prominent philosopher and mathematician, posited that animals were nothing more than complex machines devoid of feelings or consciousness[55]. This mechanistic view of nature was a stark departure from the older, more harmonious perception of the natural world as a living entity to be respected and revered.

Further, Thomas Hobbes, a political philosopher, largely regarded nature as a chaotic and brutal environment[56]. He famously said that life in the state of nature is "solitary, poor, nasty, brutish, and short." This perception of nature as a violent and unforgiving place contributed to the drive to control, dominate, and exploit it. This rhetoric, whether symbolic or not, undeniably communicated an emerging viewpoint where nature was seen not as a nurturing entity but as a subordinate, mechanical system to be exploited for human progress[57].

These views, however, were far from isolated, as the era brimmed with similar notions. John Locke, an influential Enlightenment thinker, for instance, propagated the idea that nature becomes valuable only through human labour, inherently urging exploitation[58]. Locke, developed the labour theory of property, which justified the ownership of land and natural resources based on human labour[58]. This theory further solidified the human right to exploit nature for personal gain.

Adam Smith, an 18th-century Scottish economist and philosopher, best known as the author of "The Wealth of Nations" and often regarded as the father of modern economics, viewed nature as a resource to be harnessed for economic gain[59]. Even Karl Marx, renowned for critiquing capitalism, saw nature as a material source to be transformed into commodities through human labour[60].

The age of the Industrial Revolution further accelerated this trend. Figures like James Watt and Matthew Boulton, through their development of the steam engine, dramatically amplified humanity's capacity to exploit natural resources. The philosophy of John Stuart Mill tied progress to the exploitation of natural resources, and Henry Ford's mass production techniques instigated unprecedented levels of resource consumption. By the 20th century, perspectives like Gifford Pinchot's utilitarian conservationism and Julian Simon's belief in infinite resources through human innovation continued to promote an exploitative relationship with nature.

The legacy of these influential thinkers' views, interwoven with capitalism and the scientific revolution, led to an aggressive form of exploitation of the natural world, which persists to this day. As such, it is important to consider the potential implications of this nature-human disconnect on our collective well-being.

It's crucial to clarify that these figures in our recent history aren't solely responsible for our ecological crisis. They were both catalysts for and products of larger societal transformations. Their views resonated because they echoed the emerging socio-economic conditions and zeitgeist of their times. Still, these philosophical shifts played a considerable role in framing our understanding and relationship with the natural world, ultimately contributing to our current predicament[53].

Thus, our ecological crisis is a legacy of deep-seated paradigms that sprouted centuries ago. It demands more than curtailing destructive practices; it calls for a fundamental shift in our worldview of nature. We must foster a perspective that appreciates nature's inherent value, recognising our dependence on it for survival instead of viewing it solely as a resource to exploit.

Our well-being hinges on a healthy planet. Therefore, it is essential to recalibrate our relationship with nature fundamentally[61,62]. Learning from historical missteps and reconciling our cultural and philosophical relationship with the natural world is crucial for mitigating our ecological crisis and shaping a sustainable future.

# Capitalism and the Human-Nature Disconnect

I have already mentioned capitalism several times. It is unavoidable that in examining our modern relationship with nature, it becomes apparent that capitalism, as a global socio-economic system, has greatly shaped this relationship, and unfortunately, not for the better[63]. The basic premise of capitalism, focused on ceaseless growth and expansion, has allowed the inherent competition, materialism, and egoism of human nature to manifest in ways that prove disastrous for our planet[35].

The insatiable hunger for progress and accumulation has led to the gross exploitation of natural resources. Forests are being depleted, deserts are expanding, and ecosystems are deteriorating, all in the name of industrial growth and economic development. Our focus on personal advancement, power, and wealth has resulted in practices that are blatantly unsustainable and environmentally damaging.

Further, as noted earlier, our mindset of human-exceptionalism, the belief that we are the superior species and that all others exist for our benefit, has exacerbated this ecological crisis. This belief has led to the widespread extermination of other species and the destruction of their habitats, disrupting the delicate balance of ecosystems and resulting in a loss of biodiversity. It is becoming increasingly clear that our self-centred worldview and actions are having profound consequences not just on our own health and well-being, but on the health of the planet as a whole.

In light of these realities, there is a growing call for a significant shift in our mindset and lifestyle. As argued by Marshall[64], it is paramount that we transition from competition and self-obsession towards more sustainable and collaborative ways of living. This requires us to prioritise the health of our planet and its inhabitants, recognising the intrinsic value of all life forms and their roles in maintaining the earth's ecological balance.

In the spirit of Thoreau's "all good things are wild and free," it becomes imperative for us to rewild our minds and reclaim our innate connection with the natural world. To do this, we must challenge the capitalist worldview that regards nature as a mere resource to be exploited. Instead, we must recognise and respect nature as a living, breathing entity that deserves our care and protection. Only by making this paradigm shift can we hope to restore harmony between humanity and the natural world, fostering a future that is truly wild, free, and sustainable for all life forms.

# Anthropocentrism and Urbanisation: The Root of Ecological Disconnect

The term Anthropocene, which was already briefly mentioned, rounds up everything I have noted thus far. The Anthropocene encapsulates the modern era, where human activities have been the dominant influence on the climate and the environment.

As has been argued, the Anthropocene era is characterised by significant and lasting impacts on the natural world, primarily driven by industrial processes, urbanisation, and resource extraction[65]. This term is not only a chronological designation but also embodies a profound philosophical shift in the way humans perceive their relationship with the natural world. It signifies an epoch in which humans are no longer mere spectators or passive beneficiaries of Earth's bounty but active agents in shaping its future[66].

The Anthropocene era aligns with the Enlightenment, Scientific and Industrial Revolutions, marking a significant shift in human thinking and actions towards nature. As noted previously, the Enlightenment era (1685 - 1815) heralded a period where humans began to place themselves at the centre of the universe, a notion that had far-reaching implications. This anthropocentric viewpoint spurred on by the Enlightenment facilitated a shift in the way nature was perceived and treated, from a nurturing mother to a commodity to be exploited for human gain[67].

Science and technology advanced rapidly during this time, providing the tools to exploit nature on an unprecedented scale. The Industrial Revolution amplified this effect, with the mass production of goods necessitating resource extraction at an accelerating pace. These shifts in ideology and practice were both the cause and result of the growing chasm between humans and the natural world.

This shift became more pronounced as populations began to concentrate in urban environments. Modern urbanisation trends indicate that the vast majority of people in the future will live in urban areas[68]. Living in cities can further estrange people from nature, as urban environments often lack the biodiversity and ecological richness found in more rural or wild areas. This alienation from the natural world is not merely symbolic; it has tangible effects on mental and physical health and overall quality of life[69].

Yet, we must not forget that humans are creatures of nature, evolved over millennia to live in close harmony with the natural world. The narratives of the Anthropocene and urbanisation should not lead to a fatalistic acceptance of an irrevocable disconnection from nature. Instead, they should serve as potent reminders of our need to realign our lifestyles, values, and societies with the ecological realities of our world. By doing so, we can reclaim our 'wild and free' selves, find renewed flow and harmony, and enhance our resilience in the face of the challenges presented by the modern world. This is not a regression but a progression, a necessary adaptation to a world where human and natural systems are increasingly interdependent[70].

In essence, in the throes of the Anthropocene, a reconnection with nature is not just a romantic ideal but a pragmatic and urgent necessity. It is a critical pathway to ensure a sustainable and resilient future for ourselves and the generations to come. As we navigate the complexities of the Anthropocene, the wisdom in Thoreau's words, "all good things are wild and free", should resonate deeply, guiding our steps towards a more harmonious coexistence with the natural world.

# The Mismatch Hypothesis and Urban Disconnect: A Modern Quandary

Human beings have always exhibited an ability to adapt and evolve according to environmental needs, which is one of the hallmarks of our species. However, in our rapid transition from hunter-gatherer societies to the dense urban conglomerations of today, we have far outpaced the evolutionary mechanisms that have historically allowed us to adapt. This evolutionary lag and the discordance it causes between our biology and our lifestyle is referred to as the mismatch hypothesis[71].

Introduced in the late 20th century, the mismatch hypothesis was initially used to explain the rise in 'diseases of civilisation' like heart disease, obesity, and type II diabetes, which are associated with modern lifestyles and diets[72]. It postulates that our biological systems, shaped by millions of years of evolution, are ill-equipped to handle the changes brought on by our modern environment, creating a mismatch between our genetic predispositions and current living conditions.

Our current living conditions, dominated by urban landscapes and the pressures of industrialisation and technology, starkly contrast with the natural environments our ancestors inhabited for the majority of our evolutionary history. As I have noted elsewhere, the majority of people in

Western countries now live in urban areas[73], leading to a disconnection from natural environments. The speed and scale of this transition have left little time for evolutionary adaptations to occur, leading to the issues posited by the mismatch hypothesis[74].

Implications of this hypothesis are manifold, especially in the context of mental health and well-being. Rapid urbanisation and our modern lifestyle have had profound impacts on mental health. The increase in stress-related disorders, anxiety, and depression in modern societies could be partly attributed to this mismatch[75]. There is an interesting observation here. If there was no mismatch between our current life way of living in a concrete jungle and that of our original home in nature, then spending time in nature shouldn't have any bearing on our mental health and well-being. However, there is an increasingly growing body of evidence suggesting that exposure to green spaces and nature has positive effects on mental health, reducing stress and improving mood[76]. As a result, the lack of such exposure to nature in urban environments clearly seems to exacerbate mental health issues. Let's look closer at a few others.

**Physical Health -** From a physical health perspective, our bodies evolved to be active. A sedentary lifestyle, common in city living, can lead to obesity, heart disease, and diabetes.

Our ancestors' diet consisted of lean meats, fruits, and vegetables. In contrast, modern diets are high in processed foods and sugar, leading to numerous health issues, including obesity, diabetes, and heart disease[77,78].

**Mental Health -** From a mental health perspective, the mismatch hypothesis suggests that the isolation and stress of modern city living can lead to increased rates of mental health disorders, including anxiety and depression. Our ancestors lived in close-knit communities, offering social support and shared responsibilities. The isolation of modern city living is a stark contrast and can be detrimental to mental health[79].

**Societal Structures -** The mismatch hypothesis can also be applied to societal structures. Humans evolved in egalitarian groups, whereas modern societies are often hierarchical. This can lead to power imbalances and inequality, which can cause stress and mental health issues. Moreover, the competitive nature of many modern societies may contribute to social conflict and dissatisfaction[80].

Addressing the mismatch between our biology and our environment requires a systemic approach that promotes changes at individual, societal, and environmental levels. At the individual level, this could involve making lifestyle changes, such as incorporating more physical activity into daily routines, improving diet, and reducing stress through mindfulness practices. But increasingly, and what I will be highlighting through this book, the simple act of going for a walk in a natural environment (or the closest one can get to one) is incredibly effective in aiding in better mental health and overall well-being. In doing so, we also have the opportunity to incorporate more physical activity into daily routines while reducing stress through nature-based practices.

# Rediscovering Our Indigenous Roots: Towards a Harmonious Existence with Nature

Before the dawn of modernity and the exponential expansion of cities, humans lived in intimate communion with nature. Insight into this form of existence is not entirely lost; it is still preserved in the cultures of indigenous people worldwide. Much of what I covered thus far, especially the importance of being in nature both for mental health and well-being, would seem obvious to any indigenous person.

These cultures have maintained a worldview where humans and nature are inseparable components of a holistic cosmos. As elucidated by Little Bear[81], a Blackfoot scholar, the indigenous perspective is animated by a deep sense of relationally and respect towards all forms of life. Everything in the universe is viewed as animate, imbued with spirit and knowledge, and therefore deserving of recognition and reverence as kin[81].

This all-encompassing worldview is also echoed by Yazzie, a Navajo scholar, who proposed that the Navajo's way of life is a practice of an epistemology where the human mind perceives itself as inherently connected to every aspect of the world[51]. According to Yazzie, this web of connection evokes a sense of responsibility towards nature, as nature too has its responsibilities towards humans.

Albeit this intimate and interconnected way of life seems distant and foreign to many in the developed world, growing global concerns, particularly around climate change, are pushing individuals and societies to reflect on their relationship with nature[82]. This reflection has inspired an urgent need to reconnect with the natural world, thereby breaking free from the paradigm of viewing nature solely as a resource for exploitation and dominance[83,84]. The legacy of the 19th-century mindset, which undervalued nature and perceived it as merely a tool to serve human needs, is now being critically re-evaluated.

Today's burgeoning consciousness regarding the urgent ecological crisis and the socio-emotional discomfort experienced by many in industrialised societies are paving the way towards a paradigm shift. This shift signifies a much-needed change in our perceptions and interactions with the natural world, a change that is suggestive of our yearning to return to a way of life that respects and values nature as our equal rather than our subservient.

When we observe indigenous cultures, such as the Blackfoot and Navajo, we notice a remarkable symbiotic relationship with the natural world[51]. These cultures perceive nature not merely as a separate entity or a resource, but as a community of sentient beings to which they belong[81]. This profound recognition of relationality fosters a reciprocal relationship with nature, promoting sustainability and fostering the equilibrium between human needs and environmental preservation[85].

This stark contrast between indigenous societies and the Western world reveals our deep-rooted separation from nature. A separation that is not merely physical but primarily cognitive and emotional, entrenched in our worldview that largely values the mechanical, analytical, and exploitative approach towards the environment[86].

However, we now find ourselves in a world increasingly destabilised by ecological degradation and social unrest, much of it arising from our dissociation with nature[87]. This has fostered a growing recognition of the need to reassess our position in the world and our relationship with it. As awareness increases around the ecological crisis, industrialised societies are seeking ways to reconnect with the natural world, symbolising a marked shift in global consciousness[88].

Could we look towards the wisdom of indigenous cultures to illuminate a path towards harmonious coexistence with nature? A closer look at the principles that guide these societies suggests that they might offer viable solutions to our contemporary crises. For instance, the concept of "All My Relations" deeply embedded in many indigenous cultures implies a comprehensive ethics of respect towards all life forms, an ethos that could revolutionise our relationship with nature[85].

Furthermore, the indigenous practice of gratitude, as a form of acknowledgement and reciprocity towards the natural world, can serve to foster a culture of sustainability, a significant shift from the prevalent culture of consumption and waste[85].

Finally, the indigenous recognition of place and land as a source of identity, history, and belonging provides a counter-narrative to the dominant paradigm of land as a mere commodity. This sense of place-based identity could form the basis of a deeply rooted environmental stewardship that fosters long-term commitment towards ecological preservation and restoration.

In conclusion, as we grapple with the consequences of our historical disconnect with nature, the wisdom of indigenous cultures presents us with an alternative path. This path beckons us towards a deeper, more meaningful relationship with the natural world, a relationship that recognises the interconnectedness of all life forms and honours the inherent value of the natural world. By embracing this path, we have the potential not only to resolve our ecological and socio-emotional crises but also to foster a more resilient and sustainable future.

# Coming home to our Nest

In our collective human history, the metaphorical 'nest' has represented our beginnings and our profound connection to the natural world. This connection extends far beyond the basic needs for survival – food, water, and shelter. Our 'nest' in nature also provided a sense of community and belonging, fulfilling our emotional and psychological needs, and contributing to our overall well-being[89]. This deep connection to the environment is what we have evolved from, and understanding this is pivotal for recognising why our current disconnection from nature is so impactful.

Our evolutionary journey has brought us to a place where we have seemingly outgrown our nest, creating structures, societies, and technologies far removed from the natural world. Today, we often find ourselves entangled in a web of technology and consumerism, which can result in feelings of disconnection, not just from nature, but from our intrinsic selves as well.

In this context, it's important to ask: Why was our original 'nest' so deeply connected with nature, and why didn't we evolve in an environment similar to today's world?

The evolutionary design of our 'nest' was not random. Our ancestors thrived in environments that met their biological and psychological needs, fostering a sense of community and interdependence. This is a stark contrast to our modern world, where technology often replaces genuine human connection and where the pursuit of individual success can lead to isolation[90].

So, how do we navigate this chaotic modern world without retreating to an idealised past or abandoning the world we've built? The solution lies in expanding our sense of identity and fostering a sense of interconnectedness with others. This involves embracing the shared well-being and love that arises from realising we are part of a larger whole. It's about understanding that our well-being is intrinsically tied to the well-being of others, a concept that has been explored extensively in the field of social psychology[91].

By creating a foundation based on love and interconnectedness, we can build healthier relationships with the world around us. This perspective can help us avoid the trap of demonising those who hold differing political or economic views. It can encourage us to recognise our shared humanity, even with those who may be causing harm, and to remember that such harm often stems from personal suffering or trauma.

As the sound healer Sterling Toles so poignantly puts it, "We must not only heal the suffering that oppression causes, but we must also heal all the suffering that causes oppression." This powerful sentiment highlights the necessity of addressing the root causes of oppression and harm, which often originate from deep-seated pain and suffering. Rather than responding to harm with aggression, which only perpetuates a cycle of suffering, a more potent response is to counteract harm with love, empathy, and connectivity. This approach promotes a shared sense of flourishing and fosters an environment in which everyone can thrive.

In essence, navigating the complexities and chaos of the modern world necessitates a return to our evolutionary roots. This doesn't mean physically retreating to nature, but embracing our interconnectedness with others and the natural world. It's about reigniting the sense of love that arises from this interconnectedness and leveraging it as a force for positive change in an increasingly challenging world. Bottom line, the easiest place for any of us to begin this journey is in our very own neighbourhoods, by reconnecting to the wildness that still remains right in front of us.

# Final Reflections on the Contemporary Human Condition

It is clear that as I have outlined thus far human history has been marked by a ceaseless march toward technological, societal, and political advancements, all under the banner of progress. Yet, as we pause to take stock, we find ourselves on the precipice of an unsettling reality. The edifice of modern civilisation, built on the twin pillars of capitalism and consumerism, now appears shaky and riddled with deep-seated, systemic issues. We seem to have journeyed far from our ancestral cradle, the natural world, with profound implications for our collective well-being.

Our contemporary existence is increasingly characterised by global insecurity, climate change, biodiversity loss, and a disturbing rise in mental health issues. Are we really better off than our forebears, who were intimately connected with nature and derived their sustenance and wisdom from it? The global trends and personal experiences today force us to question and reflect[92].

With the spectre of climate change looming large and concerns about ecological fallout increasing, industrialised societies have begun rethinking their relationship with nature. There's an increasing recognition that our attitude of using nature as a mere resource to be exploited, a view that, as we saw previously, became prevalent during the 1800s, needs serious revision. As scholars point out, the innate interconnections between all elements of nature, a belief long upheld by Indigenous cultures, have been largely overlooked by the West[93,88,84].

The developed world, despite seeing unprecedented prosperity and comfort over the past few decades, has not seen a corresponding rise in happiness or mental health[94]. In fact, in 26 countries, depression is the leading cause of disability. The majority of these countries fall within the so-called developed world, including the United Kingdom, Europe, and the United States, which reported moderate to high rates of depression[95].

Further, stress levels are alarmingly high. A comprehensive study commissioned by the Mental Health Foundation in 2018 reported that 74% of people in the United Kingdom felt so stressed in the past year that they were overwhelmed or unable to cope[96]. Although stress is not categorised as a mental health issue, it often triggers depression, anxiety, self-harm, suicide, and feelings of disconnection.

In the context of this prevailing discontent and unrest, a reconnection with nature presents a promising remedy. An increasing number of people, grappling with a sense of disconnection, unfulfillment, or lack of purpose, are turning to nature for solace and meaning. This sense of alienation has often been linked to rising rates of mental distress, including anxiety, depression, and burnout[94,97,98].

Nature experiences have been shown to promote mental health and well-being by reducing stress, improving mood, and fostering a sense of connection to the natural world. Moreover, nature-based interventions, such as ecotherapy which blends nature exposure with traditional forms of therapy, are being increasingly utilised to address mental health challenges[99,100]. The growing recognition of the importance of nature in promoting mental health and well-being has spurred a shift in how we think about mental health and wellness[76].

This compelling evidence underscores the urgent need for a paradigm shift from our historic disconnect from nature to a more rooted existence, aligned with the rhythms of the natural world. I believe this alignment holds immense potential for addressing the myriad issues we currently face.

The nature-human connection is not a newly discovered panacea; instead, it is a forgotten remedy. We are fundamentally creatures of nature, with our survival and evolution being intrinsically linked to the Earth and its ecosystems. Recognising this link and embracing our natural roots is an essential step toward navigating our current crises.

This connection is not a mere romantic notion; it is backed by a growing body of scientific evidence. The concept of Biophilia, introduced by biologist E.O. Wilson, posits that humans possess an innate tendency to seek connections with nature and other forms of life. Recent studies have begun to document the numerous benefits of this connection, from lower rates of mental illness to better physical health and increased longevity[101,69].

Further, time spent in natural environments has been shown to foster mindfulness, a state of being present and aware, which is linked to numerous health benefits. Mindfulness can help to reduce stress, improve cognitive function, and increase overall well-being[102].

Rekindling this bond with nature is not only good for us on an individual level but also crucial for our collective survival. Our disconnection from the natural world has led us to exploit it recklessly, leading to climate change, biodiversity loss, and various environmental crises. By rediscovering our place within the Earth's community of life, we can foster the empathy and understanding necessary to take better care of our shared home.

Despite the seemingly insurmountable challenges I've outlined so far, I'd like to impress upon you that there is hope. It's understandable if you're feeling overwhelmed or even anxious. The state of the world can often seem dire, and it's easy to become lost in a sea of despair and helplessness. But it's precisely here, in this space of recognising the gravity of our predicament, where we can find the impetus for profound change.

The question you're likely asking yourself is, "What can I do to recalibrate, to regain my health and balance in a world that seems so out of sync?" This is what we'll delve into in the sections to follow. In the pages to follow, I will be offering accessible practices that I believe can allow each of us to begin the healing journey. This begins first by healing ourselves and rediscovering our wild health, which then naturally begins to extend to all sentience on this planet. These are small steps that lead to big changes. In the end, as with anything worthwhile, you need to start somewhere, and this means starting with what is possible.

You may find it paradoxical, given the enormity of the global challenges we face, to focus on healing ourselves first. However, it's not a narcissistic endeavour but rather a necessary starting point. The truth is, to heal the world, we must begin by healing ourselves—not as an act of selfishness but as a necessity to build the inner resilience and strength that can fuel our efforts to help others and the world at large.

The good news is that deep within us, beneath layers of cultural conditioning and societal norms, exists an innate wildness—a primordial connection to the natural world. This wildness is not about being uncivilised or reckless. Instead, it's about rediscovering our natural state of being, intertwined and in harmony with the world around us. This largely forgotten state of wildness is waiting to be awakened, and reviving it can have profound implications for our personal health, our relationships with others, and the health of our planet.

In the following pages, we will explore practical ways to rekindle this wildness within us. We'll also explore the positive outcomes of embracing this forgotten state of being. Ultimately, the objective is to carry this message forward as a beacon of hope in the modern world. I have written the practices to follow in this way, explaining the myriad of benefits each practice offers, so that you can educate your friends in the same manner. We are, after all, creatures of this Earth. By aligning ourselves more closely with the natural world, we can tap into the healing, restorative powers inherent in nature and, in turn, contribute to the healing of our planet.

Understanding this doesn't only offer a fresh perspective; it provides a powerful motivation to adopt new ways of being and interacting with the world around us. We're not just individuals lost in a vast, impersonal universe; we're integral parts of a wondrous, interconnected whole. By re-establishing our bond with nature, by reclaiming our inherent wildness, we find our rightful place in the web of life—engaged, empowered, and free. And from this place, we can truly begin to make a difference.

Embracing this wildness within, this deep connection to nature, is not just an individual endeavour; it has the potential to transform societies, shift cultural norms, and influence the trajectory of our future. So, hold on to that sense of hope, because the journey we're about to embark on is not just transformative—it's essential for our survival and the well-being of our beautiful, wild, and astonishingly interconnected world.

*Wandering through nature's embrace with a loved one is like weaving our souls into the timeless tapestry of the earth.*

# The ReWild Framework

At this point, it should be clear that in the hustle and bustle of the modern world, where success is often defined by consumption, materialistic gain, competition, and an exaggerated focus on the individual, many of us have lost our innate connection with the natural world. In our race towards achieving societal expectations, we've become disconnected from ourselves and our surroundings, a disconnection often manifested as chronic discontent, restlessness, and a sense of unfulfillment. The potential solution I propose to such a predicament lies in reconnecting with nature - a healing journey that has the potential to restore our peace of mind, invigorate our senses, and revive our spirit[103,104,105].

The first step towards this transformative journey is to restore our attention to nature. It is only when we stop rushing and slow down to actually observe and interact with the world around us that we begin to truly appreciate its beauty and diversity[106]. Reconnecting with nature in this way acts as an antidote to the overwhelming stimulation of our modern lives, recharging our cognitive resources and improving our overall well-being[103,104].

Becoming present is the next step, one that asks us to fully immerse ourselves in the moment. As our minds stop darting from past regrets to future anxieties, we make space for experiencing the world as it is right now[107]. This sense of presence opens up our senses, allowing us to see, hear, smell, touch, and taste the world in a way that we often overlook in our daily routines[108,109].

As we become more attuned to our senses, we also make space for increased self-awareness. The simplicity of nature has a way of mirroring our innermost feelings, bringing to consciousness the emotions and thoughts that we have been avoiding or suppressing[105,110]. This introspection forms a critical part of the healing journey, providing the necessary clarity for us to acknowledge our anxieties and insecurities.

Next comes a sense of wholeness, a spiritual connection with nature that transcends our physical existence. We feel a unity with the world around us and realise that we are not separate entities but integral parts of an intricate web of life[111,112]. This profound realisation can fill us with a sense of awe and reverence for the natural world, evoking feelings of humility and gratitude[113].

The final stage of this transformative journey involves integrating these experiences into our daily lives. It is not enough to merely have these experiences; they must inform our interactions with the world around us, transforming us from distant observers to active participants in the natural world[114,115,116]. By engaging with nature in a meaningful and respectful way, we can reinforce our connection with it and encourage a more sustainable and empathetic approach to our environment.

From the above, nature's healing framework emerges. This is the same framework I developed through my own research into the healing power of embracing nature. It's the steps I took to bring myself back to wild health during my Covid lockdown period on the Isle of Man. I refer to it as the "ReWild Framework", consisting of 10 embodied-action steps that will guide you from a state of disconnection in the modern world to a state of profound, meaningful engagement with nature as your guide. As you work through the various practices I will be outlining in the next sections of the book, I suggest you integrate these embodied-action steps into those practices. You will find by doing so, your overall connection to the natural world will be enhanced and will allow for a deeper relationship with the natural environment itself.

**Embodied-Action Step 1 - Reconnecting to Nature:** Begin by spending time in nature, intentionally immersing yourself in your surroundings. This initial contact aims to restore your attention and pull you away from the modern world's distractions[103,104].

**Embodied-Action Step 2 - Slowing Down:** Embrace a slower pace, allowing yourself to take in the details of the natural world. By choosing to slow down, you create space to notice the rhythms and cycles of nature[106].

**Embodied-Action Step 3 - Becoming Present:** Develop mindfulness practices that anchor you in the present moment. This mindfulness aids in opening up your senses, enhancing your experience of nature[107].

**Embodied-Action Step 4 - Opening Up the Senses:** Engage all your senses in experiencing nature. Touch, smell, listen, look, and even taste, if safe and appropriate. This multi-sensory engagement allows you to become more self-aware and connected[108,109].

**Embodied-Action Step 5 - Creating Space for Self-Awareness:** By becoming aware of your inner self, you create room for unconscious thoughts and feelings to surface, enabling a deeper understanding of your psyche and emotional state[105,110].

**Embodied-Action Step 6 - Cultivating Wholeness:** Embrace a sense of oneness and unity with nature, recognising that you are part of a much larger system of life. This realisation often invokes a sense of spirituality and wonder[111].

**Embodied-Action Step 7 - Connecting to Spirit:** Engage with the spiritual dimensions of the natural world, respecting indigenous beliefs and practices that acknowledge the sacredness of nature[112].

**Embodied-Action Step 8 - Embracing Awe:** Allow yourself to be captivated by the majesty and mystery of nature, opening yourself to feelings of reverence, admiration, and awe[113].

**Embodied-Action Step 9 - Acknowledging the More-than-Human World:** Recognise and honour the existence and value of non-human entities in nature – animals, plants, rivers, mountains, etc., developing a deep respect for all forms of life[117].

**Embodied-Action Step 10 - Feeling a Sense of Belonging:** Over time, these practices can lead to a profound sense of belonging and connection, nurturing the feeling of being an integral part of the natural world rather than a separate observer[114,115,116].

Think of the ReWild Framework as a roadmap to reclaim your connection with nature and, in doing so, rediscover your own place in the world. It provides a comprehensive approach that integrates cognitive, sensory, emotional, and spiritual aspects into a holistic process of healing and growth.

Embarking on this journey of reconnection with nature can be a transformative experience, leading to a sense of peace, fulfilment, and a renewed appreciation for the beauty and wonder of the natural world. As you will see from the following practices, aspects of the ReWild Framework permeate them. At times, a few of the embodied-actions will be inherent in a practice, while at other times, you may encounter all of them in a single practice. As such, think of the ReWild Framework as invitations. An invitation to invoke as many of the embodied-action steps as possible in each practice you undertake. This, in turn, will make each practice more rewarding.

Before we get started, I want to make something clear. Yes, I have taken modernity to task in the first part of this book and for good reason. With that said, and to clarify, it isn't science and technology that I contest, but rather the paradigm that governs their application and, indeed, our broader societal functioning. This dominant worldview, underpinned by anthropocentrism, materialism, and unbridled consumerism, veils our ability to recognise our place within the world's complex network of life. We will be using technology at times in our practices, but as I noted above, it's how it is used that matters most.

Finally, it is totally up to you how you choose to

approach the following practices. You could do a different practice every day for the next 24 days or flip the book open at a random page and start with that practice. Even better, glance through the practices and choose the one that most speaks to you at this very moment. Regardless of your chosen practice, you are beginning your journey to wild health; enjoy the process.

# Practices

# Reflections on Reconnecting with Nature & Slowing Down

Before we embark on the first eight practices I will be introducing you to, let's take a moment to appreciate the magic of nature and its profound impact on our lives.

The dazzling brilliance of our modern world has its shadows. While technology has blessed us with conveniences, it's also pulled us into a whirlwind of never-ending commitments, making us feel perpetually exhausted[118]. Our bustling urban lives, with their noisy streets and flashing screens, have left many feeling mentally worn out, a sentiment echoed by multiple studies[119,120].

Enter the concept of "slow nature." Imagine a world where we pause, breathe, and truly absorb the beauty of a blossoming flower or the gentle ripples of a pond. Such moments pull us out of the race and allow us to recharge mentally and emotionally[121, 122].

Kaplan's Attention Restoration Theory (ART) beautifully illustrates this idea. It explains how the modern world's demands can wear us down, and how nature acts as a sanctuary for our overworked minds[103].

Imagine a four-part symphony: First, you feel detached from daily chaos. Next, you're mesmerised by the simplest natural wonders, like the rustling leaves. Then, you're enveloped by an expansive feeling of timelessness. Finally, you find harmony in nature's embrace[123]. These moments not only recharge us mentally but can even alleviate symptoms of mental stress[124].

But the magic doesn't end there. Nature wraps us in a cocoon of emotional warmth, reducing stress, elevating our mood, and connecting us deeply with the world around us[113,125].

So, how do we bring these blessings into our bustling city lives?

For starters, every one of us can find small ways to intertwine nature into our routines. Perhaps enjoy your lunch under the open sky or take a leisurely walk after work. Indulge in community gardening or playfully plant flowers in unexpected city spots[126].

Communities can create pockets of green, ensuring they're not just beautiful but also restorative. Imagine urban spaces where the gentle sound of water or the sight of fluttering butterflies gives our minds the break they crave[123].

But beyond individual or community actions, we need a cultural shift. Nature shouldn't be a luxury—it's our sanctuary. In times of crises, like the COVID-19 lockdowns, many found solace in the gentle embrace of green spaces[127]. It's a testament to our deep-rooted connection with the natural world.

To put it simply, in our quest for progress, let's not forget that we are born of nature. 'Slow nature' is our ally against the stresses of modern life. It's our reminder to pause, breathe, and bask in the beauty around us. As we move through the following practices, let's use them to find that precious balance between the rush of modern life and the healing embrace of nature.

**Remember:** Nature isn't an escape from modernity, but a bridge to a mentally richer life. So, as we prepare for the next practices, let's cherish and harness the healing power of nature. After all, amidst the urban hustle and bustle, we can still find our wild and free spirit. Let's begin...

# Practice 1: Concrete Jungle Safari

Turn your regular city walk into an adventure. Pretend you're on a safari, exploring the wild. Take binoculars and a camera, and document urban wildlife like birds, squirrels, insects, or even different types of trees and plants. This practice makes your everyday surroundings feel more exciting and engaging.

## Materials Needed

- A pair of binoculars or a magnifying glass.
- A camera or smartphone with a camera.
- A notepad and a pen (optional).
- A guidebook or a nature identification app on local urban wildlife, trees, and plants.

## Instructions

### Step 1: Plan Your Route

Choose a route that encompasses various urban environments, such as local parks, tree-lined streets, city gardens, and even alleyways where plants might be growing through cracks in the pavement. These are the places where you're most likely to observe urban wildlife and various plant species.

## Step 2: Gear Up

Bring along your binoculars, camera, and guidebook or nature identification app. If you're planning to record your observations, have your notepad and pen at the ready.

## Step 3: Observation

Begin your safari! As you walk, keep your eyes and ears open for signs of urban wildlife and distinctive plant life. You might spot birds perched on branches or hear them singing, squirrels scampering along fences, or insects buzzing around flowers. Examine the different types of trees and plants that you come across.

## Step 4: Documentation

When you spot something of interest, use your binoculars to get a closer look or your magnifying glass to inspect plants and insects more closely. Try to identify what you've found using your guidebook or app. Once you've identified it, take a picture for your records.

## Step 5: Reflect

Jot down your observations and reflections in your notepad. This can include the species you spotted, where and when you saw them, their behaviours, and any other interesting details. Over time, this can help you understand patterns in your urban ecosystem, such as which species are common in certain areas or at specific times of day.

**Step 6: Share Your Experience**
If you want, you can share your findings and photos with friends, family, or on social media. This can raise awareness about the biodiversity in urban environments and may inspire others to embark on their own urban safari. I know that sharing these moments is always met with joy by those who follow me on these various social platforms.

Remember, the goal of the Concrete Jungle Safari isn't about how many species you can identify or photograph, but rather about slowing down, becoming more observant, and appreciating the nature that exists within our urban environments. Take your time, be patient, and enjoy the journey as much as the findings!

# Benefits

Engaging in the Concrete Jungle Safari provides an array of benefits for your mental health and well-being, and does so in a way that encourages you to step back from the constant distractions that characterise much of modern urban life.

At the core of this practice is the promotion of

mindfulness, a state of active and open attention anchored in the present moment. In a world where an overwhelm of distractions often fragments our attention, focusing on the world around you in the context of a city safari can be a potent antidote. You'll be encouraged to slow down and notice the world around you, the chirping of birds, the rustling leaves, and the changing colours of the seasons. This practice of observation promotes a state of calm and present-moment awareness, which has been linked with decreased levels of stress and anxiety, improved focus and memory, and increased feelings of contentment and joy.

Further, the Concrete Jungle Safari invites you to stimulate your brain in a novel, engaging way. The process of identifying various species, documenting their behaviours, and observing their patterns over time requires a type of thinking that contrasts starkly with the rapid-fire, surface-level engagement typical of much technology use. This deep, focused attention can sharpen your cognitive functions, promote mental agility, and even delay cognitive aging.

As you embark on your city safari, you are also engaging in moderate physical exercise. Walking through your urban environment, even at a leisurely pace, can lead to physical health benefits like improved cardiovascular function and overall energy levels. Moreover, physical activity is closely linked with improved mood and reduced levels of stress and anxiety, contributing to a greater sense of mental well-being.

The process of engaging with your city as a naturalist would not only enhance your appreciation for the urban ecosystem, but also foster a profound sense of connection to the natural world. This connection can bring about a heightened sense of peace and contentment and a greater appreciation for the beauty that can be found in the everyday. This sense of being a part of something bigger can lead to increased feelings of happiness and satisfaction.

By documenting your observations and findings, whether through sketches, written descriptions or simple mental notes, you engage your creative side, providing an outlet for self-expression and a chance to see the world through an artistic lens. Engaging in creative pursuits like this has been associated with improved mental health, increased feelings of relaxation and happiness, and a reduction in stress and anxiety.

Finally, embarking on a Concrete Jungle Safari provides a profound sense of achievement. The thrill of identifying a new species or understanding a previously observed pattern in urban wildlife behaviours offers a sense of accomplishment that can boost your self-confidence and self-esteem. Over time, these small victories can contribute to a greater sense of purpose and a deeper connection to your urban environment.

In conclusion, the Concrete Jungle Safari invites you to disconnect from the fast pace of urban life and reconnect with the natural world around you. In doing so, it provides a host of mental and physical health benefits, all while fostering a greater appreciation for the hidden wonders of our urban environments.

*I took this photo of Brassica fruticulosa Cirillo, also known as Wild turnip, right outside the doorstep of my apartment building on one of my Concrete Jungle Safari outings. The fun part is that I didn't know it was edible at the time I took the photo.*

# Practice 2: Nature's Art Gallery

Choose a quiet spot in a nearby park or garden, and bring your sketchbook and pencils or paints. Try to capture the beauty of nature through drawing or painting. The focus required to create art can offer a great way to slow down, and you'll likely find a new appreciation for your local flora and fauna.

## Materials Needed

- A sketchbook or a canvas.
- Art supplies like pencils, charcoal, pastels, watercolours, or acrylic paints.
- A comfortable chair or blanket to sit on.
- A water bottle if using watercolours.

## Instructions

### Step 1: Choose Your Location

Find a quiet, comfortable spot in a local park, garden, or even your backyard. Look for a place that offers a good view of interesting natural subjects such as trees, flowers, a pond, or wildlife.

### Step 2: Set Up Your Space

Once you've chosen your location, set up your art station. Lay out your sketchbook or canvas, art supplies, and water bottle if you're using watercolours. Ensure you're comfortable, as you may be sitting here for a while.

### Step 3: Select Your Subject

Look around and select a subject for your artwork. It might be a particular tree that stands out, a bed of flowers, a beautiful bird, or a captivating landscape view. Choose something that inspires you.

### Step 4: Observe and Begin Sketching

Take a moment to really observe your subject. Notice the shapes, colours, textures, and patterns. Once you have a good mental image, start sketching or painting. If you're drawing, begin with the overall shapes before moving on to the details. If you're painting, start by laying down the broader strokes of colour before adding finer details.

### Step 5: Be Patient and Enjoy the Process

Creating art requires patience. If it doesn't look perfect right away, that's okay. The goal isn't necessarily to create a masterpiece, but to slow down, engage deeply with the natural world around you, and express your experiences through art. Enjoy the process of observing, interpreting, and creating.

**Step 6: Reflect and Share**

Once you're done, take a moment to reflect on the experience. How do you feel? What did you notice about your subject that you hadn't seen before? If you're comfortable, consider sharing your artwork and your experiences with others, either in person or on social media.

The "Nature's Art Gallery" practice not only encourages slowing down and connecting with nature but also fosters creativity and provides a tangible record of your experiences in the natural world.

# Benefits

Embarking on the "Nature's Art Gallery" practice nurtures a profound connection with the natural world around you, inviting a refreshing escape from our technology-driven routines and providing ample benefits for your mental health and overall well-being.

At the heart of this activity is the promotion of mindfulness, similar to the Concrete Jungle Safari, but with a distinct, artistic twist. As you sit in your chosen location and immerse yourself in sketching or painting, you inherently shift your focus from daily stressors to gentle brush strokes depicting the intricate beauty of nature. This intense focus on the present moment can help reduce feelings of stress and anxiety, improving your overall mood and creating a sense of inner calm. This quiet, contemplative time spent with nature and your sketchbook can also help rejuvenate your mind, providing a refreshing break from the cognitive demands of urban life.

In addition to mindfulness, the practice of creating art from nature can provide a sense of accomplishment and self-confidence. Each stroke of the brush or pencil, each interpretation of natural beauty, is a testament to your creativity and patience. Regardless of the final product, the process itself offers a meaningful sense of achievement that can help boost your self-esteem. Moreover, creating art encourages self-expression, allowing you to interpret and convey your emotions in a unique and personal way. This form of self-expression has been linked to a stronger sense of identity and improved emotional well-being.

Beyond the personal benefits, creating art in nature also fosters a deep appreciation and understanding of the natural world. Observing the intricate details of a flower, the patterns of a bird's feather, or the varying shades of green in a tree's leaves can cultivate a newfound admiration for the complexity and beauty of our environment. This sense of appreciation can contribute to feelings of contentment and happiness and may even inspire a greater commitment to environmental stewardship.

As you continue with this practice, you might also discover a newfound patience. Art creation, like nature, cannot be rushed. It requires a willingness to slow down, to spend time with your subject, and gradually bring your vision to life. This patience can be a valuable trait to carry into other aspects of life, contributing to a more balanced, less stressful daily routine.

In conclusion, the "Nature's Art Gallery" practice offers a unique blend of mindfulness, creativity, and nature appreciation. It encourages you to disconnect from the fast pace of urban life, to engage deeply with the natural world, and to express your experiences in a tangible form. The benefits of this practice extend beyond the canvas or sketchbook, fostering a greater sense of calm, self-esteem, and connection with nature that can enhance your overall well-being.

# Practice 3: Urban Foraging

With a little research on edible plants in your area, take a walk and identify these species. Not only does this allow you to engage with nature in a new way, but it's also an opportunity to learn about local plant life and introduce a new hobby. Remember, always ensure that you have correctly identified plants before consuming them and that they are safe and legal to pick.

## Materials Needed

- A good quality, up-to-date field guide to edible plants in your area.
- A basket or bag for collecting.
- Gloves to protect your hands while picking.
- A knife or pair of scissors for cutting plants.

## Instructions

### Step 1: Prepare and Research

Before you start urban foraging, you need to do some research. Invest in a quality field guide for edible plants in your region and spend some time learning about what's safe to pick and eat. Some common edible plants in urban areas include dandelions and berries, but this can vary widely based on your location. For example, on the Isle of Man, where I live, blackberries, when in season, can be found island-wide.

### Step 2: Plan Your Route
Choose a route that passes through areas with lots of plant life. This could be a local park, a quiet street lined with trees, or even your own backyard.

### Step 3: Start Your Adventure
Once you're ready to start foraging, head out with your basket or bag, gloves, and knife or scissors. Keep your field guide close at hand for reference.

### Step 4: Identify and Collect
As you walk, look for the plants you've identified in your field guide. Be careful to positively identify each plant before picking. If you're in doubt, don't pick it.

### Step 5: Be Mindful of Rules and Safety
Always ensure it's legal and ethical to forage in the area you've chosen. Avoid foraging by busy roads or in areas that may have been treated with pesticides or other chemicals. Never pick a plant that's rare or protected.

### Step 6: Enjoy Your Harvest

Once you've collected some edible plants, take them home and enjoy! You can use them in cooking, make herbal teas, or even create homemade remedies.

Remember, the goal of "Urban Foraging" isn't just to collect plants, but to engage more deeply with nature, to learn about the plant life in your area, and to take time to slow down and enjoy the experience. Always be respectful of nature, and only take what you need. Happy foraging!

# Benefits

Urban Foraging offers a unique way to connect with nature right in your city, providing a range of benefits that can greatly enhance your mental well-being and overall health.

First and foremost, this practice promotes a sense of mindfulness, akin to the practices of Concrete Jungle Safari and Nature's Art Gallery, but with a culinary twist. As you learn to identify different plants and navigate your surroundings, your focus is drawn away from the usual urban distractions and towards the present moment. This focus on the here and now helps to reduce feelings of stress and anxiety, fostering an overall sense of peace and calm. This heightened sense of awareness of your environment can also make you more attuned to the beauty and intricacies of the world around you, contributing to a sense of joy and contentment.

Additionally, the act of foraging stimulates cognitive function in a novel and engaging way. The process of learning about different plant species, identifying them in the wild, and understanding their culinary uses encourages analytical thinking, memory recall, and problem-solving skills. Engaging your brain in such a manner can boost mental agility, sharpen memory, and improve focus.

Urban Foraging also enables a deeper connection with the environment, fostering a sense of respect and stewardship towards the natural world. This sense of connection can elicit feelings of satisfaction and belonging, which have been linked with improved mental well-being. Understanding and appreciating the wealth of resources that nature provides within our urban settings can foster a profound sense of gratitude, which is a key component of happiness and overall life satisfaction.

The practice of foraging not only provides a sense of mental and emotional enrichment, but can also contribute to physical health. Walking through your urban environment, searching for edible plants, provides a form of light exercise that, while not as intense as a full workout, still offers benefits such as improved cardiovascular health, enhanced mood, and increased energy levels.

Finally, the tangible reward of your foraging - the edible plants you've gathered - introduces a unique element of joy to the process. Whether you're incorporating your finds into a delicious meal, brewing them into a soothing herbal tea, or creating homemade remedies, there's a tangible satisfaction in using what you've personally gathered from nature. This not only provides a great sense of accomplishment but can also inspire a newfound interest in cooking and nutrition, further enhancing your overall well-being.

In essence, the practice of "Urban Foraging" invites you to interact with your environment in a uniquely engaging and rewarding way. The practice fosters mindfulness, cognitive stimulation, physical activity, environmental stewardship, and culinary creativity, all contributing to a deeper connection with the natural world and improved mental and physical well-being.

*Blackberry season on the Isle of Man is one of my favourite times to forage.*

# Practice 4: Guerrilla Gardening

Brighten up urban spaces by secretly planting flowers or small plants in forgotten urban spots. It's a fun and rewarding activity that brings more greenery to the city. Always remember to respect public spaces and plant responsibly.

## Materials Needed

- Seedlings or seeds of hardy, non-invasive plants suitable for your local climate.
- A trowel or small shovel for digging.
- Gloves to protect your hands.
- A watering can or bottle.
- Optional: compost or fertiliser.

## Instructions

### Step 1: Choose Suitable Plants

Choose plants that are hardy and suitable for your local climate. Native plants are often a good choice as they are more likely to thrive and less likely to harm local ecosystems. If using seeds, consider seed bombs – small balls of compost and seeds which can be easily tossed into hard to reach places.

**Step 2: Select Your Spot**

Select an unloved spot that could use some greenery. This could be a barren patch of dirt by the sidewalk, a neglected planter, or even a roundabout. Be respectful of public and private properties. Never plant on land that is being actively maintained or could disrupt local wildlife or plants.

**Step 3: Prepare the Area**

Using your gloves and trowel or small shovel, prepare the area by removing any trash and loosening the soil.

**Step 4: Planting**

Place your seedling or seeds in the soil. If you're using a seedling, dig a hole deep enough for the roots. For seeds or seed bombs, follow the planting instructions for the specific plant.

**Step 5: Care for Your Plant**

Once planted, water your plant thoroughly and if you have, add a small amount of compost or fertiliser to give it a good start.

**Step 6: Check-In**

Regularly check on your plant, especially in the beginning.

If the weather is dry, you might need to water it.

**Step 7: Watch It Grow**

Over time, watch your guerrilla garden flourish and bring a bit of nature to the city.

Remember, the aim of Guerrilla Gardening is not just to beautify urban spaces, but to engage with nature and bring awareness to the importance of green spaces in urban environments. Always be respectful of nature and public spaces. Happy gardening!

# Benefits

The practice of "Guerrilla Gardening" serves as a creative and proactive means of integrating nature into urban life, offering a variety of benefits for mental health and overall well-being.

This activity promotes a deep sense of engagement and connection with nature. As you scout out locations, select plants, and observe your green additions to the urban landscape grow and thrive, you develop a greater appreciation for the intricacies and beauty of the natural world. This appreciation can help cultivate a sense of peace and tranquillity, which can serve as a counterbalance to the hustle and bustle of city life. Numerous studies have shown that such engagement with nature can significantly reduce stress, improve mood, and boost overall psychological well-being.

Guerrilla Gardening can also foster a sense of responsibility and stewardship. The act of planting and caring for your plants can imbue a feeling of purpose and commitment. This sense of responsibility, particularly towards the environment, can encourage feelings of empowerment, resilience, and self-efficacy. These feelings can translate into a variety of positive mental health outcomes, including reduced symptoms of depression and anxiety.

Engaging in this practice also stimulates creativity. The process of choosing the right plants, deciding where to plant them, and imagining how they will enhance the space, requires imagination and innovative thinking. This creative exercise can boost cognitive function, enhance problem-solving skills, and stimulate the release of dopamine, a neurotransmitter associated with pleasure and satisfaction.

Moreover, Guerrilla Gardening can increase social connections and foster a sense of community. By beautifying shared urban spaces, you are contributing to the collective well-being. This can help establish a sense of belonging and connectedness, factors that are known to contribute to positive mental health and can lead to greater happiness and satisfaction with life.

Lastly, Guerrilla Gardening encourages physical activity. From scouting locations, preparing the soil, planting, and caring for your plants, each step of the process involves moderate physical exertion. Regular physical activity is known to help reduce the risk of a variety of health issues, improve mood, boost energy levels, and promote better sleep.

In essence, Guerrilla Gardening is not only a fun and creative activity but also a rewarding practice that can enhance mental health, stimulate physical activity, foster a sense of responsibility and stewardship, stimulate creativity, and build community, all while beautifying our urban landscapes.

# Practice 6: Mindful Photography

Use your phone camera or a digital camera to capture the elements of nature you find around the city. Look for details, patterns, and colours that catch your eye. This practice helps you to slow down and truly see the beauty that can be found in urban nature.

## Materials Needed

- A camera – this could be a professional digital camera or simply the camera on your smartphone.
- Comfortable shoes for walking.
- Optional: A notebook and pen for jotting down thoughts or observations.

## Instructions

### Step 1: Set an Intention

Before you begin, set an intention for your mindful photography session. This could be to appreciate the small details, to notice the colours of nature, or simply to be present in the moment. This helps to focus your mind and sets a positive tone for your practice.

**Step 2: Choose Your Route**

Select a route for your walk. This could be a favourite path in a city park, a tree-lined street, or even a busy urban area with small green spaces. Remember, the goal is not to find perfect beauty but to notice and appreciate the natural elements in your everyday environment.

**Step 3: Begin Your Walk**

Begin your walk, moving slowly and deliberately. Pay attention to your surroundings. Notice the colours, the light, and the way plants grow from the cracks in the pavement or climb up the walls of buildings. Be fully present in the moment, observing the nature around you.

**Step 4: Capture Your Observations**

When something catches your eye, stop and take a moment to truly see it. Notice its colours, textures, and the way it fits into its surroundings. Then, capture this moment with your camera. Don't rush this process, and don't worry about taking 'perfect' photos. This practice is about the process of seeing, not the outcome.

**Step 5: Reflect**

After taking each photo, you might want to take a moment to jot down a few thoughts or observations about it. What did you notice? What did you appreciate about this element of nature?

**Step 6: Review and Appreciate**

Once you've finished your walk, take some time to look through your photos. Notice any themes or patterns. Appreciate the beauty you've been able to observe and capture.

Mindful Photography can be a powerful way to engage with nature, even in urban environments. Through this practice, you can learn to slow down, observe, and appreciate the natural beauty that is all around you, if only you take the time to see it.

# Benefits

In an urban setting, it's easy to lose touch with the beauty of nature that surrounds us. Our attention is often captured by the rhythm of city life, making us oblivious to the small details that subtly stitch the fabric of nature into our daily environment. But, with a gentle shift in perspective, it's possible to rekindle a sense of awe and appreciation for nature, even in the heart of a concrete jungle. One such practice that can help you achieve this is Mindful Photography, I know it has for me.

Mindful Photography encourages you to embrace the present moment, using the simple tool of a camera, be it a sophisticated DSLR or just your smartphone's camera. It's not so much about the quality of the photographs you take, but rather the quality of the attention you pay to your surroundings. By focusing on capturing images of the natural world around you, it's a way of 'seeing' and deeply appreciating the often unnoticed details of urban life - the rustling leaves in a park, a vibrant sunset over rooftops, or flowers sprouting in the most unexpected places. This act of keen observation and 'seeing' can have profound effects on your mental well-being.

Not only does this practice foster mindfulness and presence, but it also cultivates a sense of gratitude for the beauty that nature offers us, even amidst the steel and concrete. Over time, this can lead to increased feelings of contentment and happiness. It's a unique form of meditation where the act of looking through a lens can help you to focus, to see beyond the obvious, and to capture a moment of natural beauty in its purest form.

Furthermore, as you embark on your walks with the intention of practising Mindful Photography, you'll be engaging in a form of light physical activity, which is known to boost your mood and relieve stress. The act of walking, exploring, and discovering can create a sense of adventure and play, which is a vital aspect of maintaining psychological well-being.

Lastly, the process of reviewing your photos can provide a sense of accomplishment, reinforcing the positive aspects of the practice. By reflecting on the images you've captured, you not only admire nature's beauty from a new perspective, but you also have the opportunity to observe any themes or patterns that emerge. This process of reflection can lead to greater self-awareness and an enriched understanding of your personal connections to the world around you.

In conclusion, Mindful Photography, as a practice, can act as a gentle, yet powerful tool for boosting your mental health and well-being. By nudging you to slow down, observe, and appreciate the beauty in everyday urban life, it offers a pathway to a more mindful and grateful way of living.

*During one of my walks in Douglas, the 'city centre' of the Isle of Man, I photographed a black snail beetle. I spent an entire month having fun capturing often-overlooked aspects of nature in our midst.*

# Practice 7: Pavement Poet

Take some chalk with you and find a quiet spot in a park or near a tree. Let nature inspire you to write a poem or a short story, then write it on the pavement for others to enjoy. This combines creativity with a connection to nature, providing a unique way to slow down.

## Materials Needed

- Chalk – ideally multiple colours, but one will do just fine.
- Comfortable clothes suitable for sitting on the pavement.
- A notebook and pen for drafting your thoughts (optional).

## Instructions

### Step 1: Choose Your Spot
Find a quiet spot in a park, near a tree, or any other place that inspires you and has a suitable surface for chalk. Make sure that it's a place where chalking is permitted, and remember to respect public and private properties.

## Step 2: Connect with Nature

Spend some time connecting with nature. You could do this by taking a few moments to quietly observe your surroundings, listen to the natural sounds, or close your eyes and breathe in the fresh air. Pay attention to how you feel during these moments.

## Step 3: Let Inspiration Strike

Think about what you've observed and how it makes you feel. Then, let nature inspire you to write a poem or a short story. It doesn't have to rhyme or follow any specific format - the most important thing is that it's a reflection of your personal connection with nature.

## Step 4: Write it Down

Once you've formed your poem or story, write it down with your chalk. Remember, this is not about creating a perfect piece of art, but about expressing your thoughts and feelings in a unique and creative way. If you prefer, you can draft your work in your notebook first, then transcribe it onto the pavement.

## Step 5: Share with Others

Leave your work for others to enjoy. Who knows, your words might inspire someone else to slow down and connect with nature too!

"Pavement Poet" is an interactive way to express your creativity while deepening your connection with nature. It allows you to engage with your surroundings in a novel and mindful way, promoting slowing down and focusing on the present moment.

# Benefits

Urban environments are often buzzing with noise, activity, and constant motion. Amidst this ceaseless hustle and bustle, it's easy to lose touch with our inherent creative nature and the calming influence of the natural world around us. An engaging and creative practice that can help you reconnect with both of these elements is the Pavement Poet.

At its core, Pavement Poet involves a unique interplay of creativity and nature appreciation. You spend time in a quiet urban green space, soak in its ambiance, and then use chalk to share your reflections on the pavement in the form of a poem or a short story. This mindful engagement with the environment fosters deepened connections with nature, even in the heart of the city, which is beneficial for your mental health and well-being.

The simple act of observing the details of your surroundings - the rustle of leaves, the flight of a bird, the silhouette of a tree against the sky - can help foster mindfulness. This state of active, open attention on the present is known to reduce stress, enhance emotional well-being, and improve overall mental health.

In terms of creativity, this practice encourages self-expression in a very accessible, spontaneous way. Writing your thoughts and impressions in the form of a poem or a short story is a form of self-exploration that can provide emotional catharsis and contribute to a greater sense of peace and understanding. Expressive writing has been shown in various studies to have therapeutic benefits, including reducing feelings of anxiety and depression.

The Pavement Poet practice also has a social component. By leaving your words on the pavement, you're sharing a piece of yourself with others. This act of sharing your thoughts and feelings can provide a sense of connectedness, enhancing feelings of belonging and reducing feelings of isolation. Plus, your creativity might spark joy, intrigue, or inspiration in others, positively affecting their day in unexpected ways.

Lastly, the simple act of sitting quietly and writing can provide a much-needed opportunity to slow down. The slower pace can counteract the fast rhythm of city life, providing balance and helping to cultivate peace of mind.

In conclusion, the practice of Pavement Poet is a simple yet profound way to enhance your mental wellbeing.

It combines the benefits of nature appreciation, creativity, mindfulness, and community engagement, offering a refreshing pause in the urban hustle. So, grab a piece of chalk and let your creative spirit be inspired by the nature around you.

# Practice 8: Green Spaces Explorer

Make it your mission to visit all the green spaces in your city. It could be parks, community gardens, or even green rooftops. Rate them based on their tranquillity, the diversity of plants, and the availability of spots to sit and relax. You might discover some hidden gems in the process.

## Materials Needed

- A local map or GPS-enabled device.
- Comfortable walking shoes.
- A notebook and pen to document your findings.
- A camera to capture the beauty of each space (optional).

## Instructions

### Step 1: Research Green Spaces in Your Area

Begin by conducting a little research on the green spaces in your city. This might include public parks, community gardens, green rooftops, or even cemeteries. Make a list or mark them on a map.

**Step 2: Plan Your Route**

After you've identified all the green spaces in your city, plan your route. You can choose to visit them based on their proximity, size, or any other criteria that appeals to you. Make sure to wear comfortable shoes as there could be a lot of walking involved.

**Step 3: Exploration Time**

Visit each green space and take the time to truly experience it. Walk around, sit and relax, observe the diversity of plant life, and notice the sounds and smells. Take photos if you'd like, but most importantly, be present and enjoy the experience.

**Step 4: Rate Your Experience**

After visiting each space, rate your experience. You could use criteria like tranquillity, diversity of plants, availability of quiet spots to sit and relax, cleanliness, or any other factors that are important to you. Write down your thoughts in your notebook.

**Step 5: Reflect and Share**

After you've visited all the green spaces, reflect on your experience. Did you discover any hidden gems? Were there any spaces that you particularly liked or disliked? Share your experiences with friends, family, or on social media.

You might inspire others to become Green Spaces Explorers too!

Remember, the goal of "Green Spaces Explorer" is not just to explore the green spaces in your city but also to slow down, spend time in nature, and appreciate the natural beauty in urban environments.

# Benefits

Engaging in the Green Spaces Explorer practice offers a multitude of benefits that contribute to both mental and physical well-being. As you embark on a mission to visit all the green spaces in your city, you open yourself up to a unique and enriching experience that goes beyond mere sightseeing.

One of the significant advantages of this practice is stress reduction. Green spaces, such as parks and community gardens, provide a serene and calming environment that allows you to escape the hustle and bustle of city life. The tranquillity of these natural settings, coupled with the soothing sounds of nature, helps to lower stress levels and promote relaxation.

Exploring green spaces also fosters a deeper connection with nature. In today's fast-paced urban world, many people feel disconnected from the natural world.

However, by immersing yourself in these green oases, you get the opportunity to appreciate the beauty of nature in an urban environment. This reconnection with nature has been shown to improve overall mood and mental well-being.

The act of exploring and experiencing different green spaces encourages mindfulness and presence. As you walk among the diverse plants, sit and relax in these peaceful surroundings, and observe the sights and sounds, you become more attuned to the present moment. This mindfulness practice brings a sense of grounding and helps to alleviate anxiety.

In addition to the mental benefits, the Green Spaces Explorer practice also provides physical activity. Walking from one green space to another is a gentle form of exercise that promotes better physical health. The combination of fresh air, gentle movement, and exposure to nature contributes to a holistic sense of well-being.

Moreover, the practice stimulates creativity and inspiration. The natural beauty of these green spaces can ignite your imagination and encourage creative thinking. You might find yourself inspired to write, sketch, or take photographs, further enhancing the experience.

Another advantage of this practice is the opportunity for community connection. During your explorations, you may encounter like-minded individuals or groups who share a passion for nature and urban green spaces.

Engaging in conversations with fellow explorers can lead to new friendships and a sense of belonging within your community.

Furthermore, the Green Spaces Explorer practice cultivates environmental awareness. As you witness the beauty and significance of these green areas, you become more conscious of the need to preserve and protect them. This increased environmental awareness may influence more sustainable practices in your daily life.

Reflecting on your experiences and sharing them with others can be rewarding in itself. By discussing your discoveries, you might inspire friends, family, or social media followers to embark on their own Green Spaces Explorer journey, fostering a collective appreciation for urban nature.

In conclusion, the Green Spaces Explorer practice offers a range of benefits that contribute to a healthier and more mindful lifestyle. By embracing the natural beauty of green spaces within the city, you can enhance your mental well-being, foster a deeper connection with nature, and find solace in the midst of urban life. So put on your comfortable walking shoes, grab a map, and embark on this enriching journey to discover the hidden gems of your city's green spaces.

*Summerhill Glen in Douglas, Isle of Man. This glen is a hidden gem right in the heart of urban sprawl, filled with streams and footpaths to explore.*

# Reflections on Being Present, Opening up The Senses & Self-Awareness

In practices 9 to 14, you will learn how to fully embrace the present moment, enliven your senses, and discover the journey of self-awareness. But first, let's unravel what it means to truly connect with nature amidst the city's hustle and bustle.

Have you ever felt lost in the constant buzz of notifications, tasks, and information? You're not alone. The modern world's fast-paced nature can sometimes blur our real-time experience of life, making it feel like we're watching a movie on fast-forward[128]. The good news? Nature, with its gentle whispers and steady rhythm, can be our anchor to the present.

Mindfulness is often described as the act of being present, immersed in the now, and seeing things without judgment[129,130]. In simpler terms, it's about experiencing life without being caught up in our thoughts, without letting yesterday's regrets or tomorrow's anxieties cloud our vision. Imagine watching a bird fly without narrating its journey in your mind; that's mindfulness.

One fascinating aspect of mindfulness is 'decentering,' which means viewing our thoughts and emotions as fleeting moments rather than defining truths[131]. It's like watching clouds pass by; we observe without getting attached.

Here's something to ponder: our minds often wander, reminiscing about the past or dreaming of the future, which can disconnect us from the present[132]. Nature and mindfulness, when combined, act as a bridge, reconnecting us with the now.

Let's be real. The urban chaos, with its neon lights and traffic noise, can make tuning into nature seem challenging. Yet, the magic of nature, be it the song of birds or the dance of leaves, offers us a unique sensory feast[133]. This multisensory experience invites our mind to sync with nature's rhythm, paving the way for a clearer mindset and enhanced well-being[134,131].

But how do you find nature in a concrete jungle? Start simple. Take a moment each day to feel the sun on your face, walk barefoot on the grass in a park, or nurture a plant on your windowsill[135]. The key is to be present during these pockets of nature experiences.

Embracing mindfulness not only enriches our personal journey but holds promise for our planet. By fostering a deeper connection with nature, we become more eco-conscious and make choices that benefit Mother Earth[136].

To wrap up, slowing down and relishing nature's wonders promises a renewed sense of self and an enriched connection with the environment. Amid the whirlwind of modern life, let's remember to pause, breathe in nature's beauty, and immerse ourselves in the present. In this conscious connection, we discover a reservoir of strength and serenity. Now for the practices.

# Practice 9: Mindful Observation

Choose a spot in your local park or green space and sit quietly, observing the natural elements around you. Watch the movement of leaves, listen to the rustling of trees, the chirping of birds, or simply notice the varying shades of green. Practising this mindful observation can help you focus on the present moment and foster a sense of connection with the environment.

### Step 1: Find a Suitable Spot

Choose a quiet and comfortable spot in a nearby park or green space where you can sit undisturbed for a while. Look for a place with natural elements like trees, plants, or a view of the sky.

### Step 2: Get into a Comfortable Position

Sit in a posture that is relaxed and sustainable for the duration of the practice. You can choose to sit cross-legged on the ground or use a cushion or bench for support. Keep your back straight but not tense, and rest your hands comfortably on your lap or thighs.

### Step 3: Set Your Intention

Take a moment to set your intention for this practice. Remind yourself that the purpose is to cultivate mindfulness, presence, and a deeper connection with the natural environment. Let go of any expectations or judgments and approach this experience with an open mind.

**Step 4: Engage your Senses**

Begin by taking a few deep breaths to centre yourself. Then, start to bring your attention to your senses. Notice the sounds around you – the rustling of leaves, bird songs, or any other natural sounds. Allow the sounds to come and go without getting caught up in them.

**Step 5: Shift your Focus**

Now, shift your attention to the sights around you. Gently scan the environment and observe the colours, shapes, and movements of the natural elements. Notice the play of light and shadow, the textures of the leaves or grass, and any small details that capture your attention.

**Step 6: Be Present with the Experience**

As you observe the natural elements, stay fully present with the experience. Resist the urge to analyse or label what you see. Instead, simply notice and accept each sight as it arises, allowing your awareness to rest on each object or scene for a few moments before moving on.

**Step 7: Return to the Breath**

If you find your mind wandering or getting caught up in thoughts, gently bring your attention back to your breath. Use the breath as an anchor to help you stay rooted in the present moment.

**Step 8: Practice Non-Judgment**

Throughout the observation, practice non-judgment. Avoid labelling the sights as good or bad, beautiful or ugly. Instead, cultivate a sense of curiosity and openness, embracing the experience just as it is.

**Step 9: Conclude the Practice**

After spending some time in mindful observation, take a moment to express gratitude for the opportunity to connect with nature. Slowly transition back to your surroundings, gently bringing your attention back to your body and the present moment.

Remember, the goal of this practice is not to achieve a particular outcome but to cultivate mindfulness and deepen your connection with the natural world. Enjoy the process of observing and being present in the beauty of nature.

# **Benefits**

In the midst of our fast-paced and often chaotic lives, connecting with the simplicity and serenity of nature can provide much-needed calmness and clarity. This is the purpose behind the "Mindful Observation" practice.

Mindful Observation is a powerful practice that invites you to intentionally engage with the natural world around you. By observing the environment with non-judgmental awareness, you open yourself up to experience the present moment fully, fostering a deeper sense of connection with nature and promoting mental wellness.

The beauty of this practice lies in its simplicity. All you need is a comfortable spot outdoors and a willingness to experience the world as it is, without preconceived ideas or judgments. By doing so, you tap into the numerous mental health benefits associated with mindfulness and nature.

To start with, research suggests that mindfulness can reduce stress, anxiety, and depression while improving overall wellbeing and life satisfaction. By focusing your attention on the present moment and accepting it without judgment, you can break away from negative thought patterns and cultivate a sense of peace and calm.

Moreover, mindfulness can help improve focus and concentration. The act of attentively observing your surroundings strengthens your ability to maintain attention and ignore distractions, which can translate to other areas of your life as well.

Beyond mindfulness, simply spending time in nature also has numerous mental health benefits. Research shows that nature can lower levels of cortisol (a stress hormone), reduce feelings of fatigue, and boost mood. Furthermore, being in green spaces can foster a sense of awe, which has been linked to increased happiness and decreased inflammation.

Through Mindful Observation, you can also cultivate a greater sense of connection with the environment. This practice reminds us that we are part of a larger ecosystem, fostering a sense of belonging and helping to alleviate feelings of loneliness and isolation.

Moreover, by tuning into the sights, sounds, and textures of the natural world, you engage your senses in a way that can bring about a sense of joy and curiosity. It encourages you to appreciate the beauty and complexity of the natural world, fostering a sense of gratitude.

In summary, the Mindful Observation practice is an invitation to slow down, immerse yourself in the natural world, and reconnect with the present moment. It is a beautiful blend of mindfulness and ecotherapy that encourages mental well-being and fosters a profound sense of connection with the environment around us. So, find a comfortable spot outdoors, quiet your mind, open your senses, and delve into the experience of simply being.

*I took this photo in the early morning of a group of birds enjoying a puddle party on a paved area opposite the Deichman Bjørvika library in Oslo, Norway. As I sat there, it brought me immense joy to watch them dance in the water. Yet, I noticed how many people, in their rush to the office, missed this simple spectacle.*

# Practice 10: Nature Journaling

Take a notebook and pen to your favourite natural space in the city and write down what you observe, feel, smell, hear, and see. It's a great way to concentrate on the 'now' and truly appreciate your surroundings. You could even sketch or paint what you see, further enhancing your mindfulness. Here is a step-by-step guide to begin journaling.

# Instructions

### Step 1: Choose Your Natural Space
Select your favourite natural spot in the city, such as a park, garden, or tree-lined street. Find a place that resonates with you and offers a sense of tranquillity and connection to nature.

### Step 2: Gather Your Journaling Materials
Take a notebook or journal and a pen or pencil with you. You may also consider bringing coloured pencils or paints if you enjoy adding visual elements to your journal.

## Step 3: Settle into the Environment

Find a comfortable spot to sit or stand in your chosen natural space. Take a few moments to ground yourself and become present in your surroundings. Take a few deep breaths to relax and centre your mind.

## Step 4: Engage Your Senses

Begin by focusing on your senses. Notice the sounds around you – the rustling of leaves, bird calls, or the hum of insects. Take in the scents in the air – the fragrance of flowers, the earthiness of the soil, or the freshness of the breeze. Feel the textures around you – the roughness of tree bark, the softness of grass, or the smoothness of a stone. Engage all your senses to fully immerse yourself in the present moment.

## Step 5: Observe and Describe

Start writing in your journal, describing what you observe and experience in detail. Write down the sights, sounds, smells, textures, and any other sensory impressions that capture your attention. Use descriptive language to bring your experience to life on the pages of your journal.

**Step 6: Express Your Feelings**

Reflect on how being in nature makes you feel. Describe your emotions, sensations, and any insights or inspirations that arise during your time in the natural environment. Allow your journal to become a space for self-expression and self-reflection.

**Step 7: Capture the Visuals**

If you feel inclined, sketch or paint what you see in your natural surroundings. You don't have to be an artist – the purpose is to engage with the visual elements and capture them in your own unique way. Let your creativity flow and don't worry about perfection.

**Step 8: Take Your Time**

Spend as much time as you need in your chosen natural space. Allow yourself to be fully present, taking in the details and immersing yourself in the experience. There is no rush – this is your time to slow down and savour the moment.

**Step 9: Reflect and Conclude**

Before leaving the natural space, take a few moments to reflect on your journaling experience. Consider what you have learned, how you have connected with nature, and the impact it has had on your state of mind. Express gratitude for the opportunity to be present in nature and engage in this mindful practice.

Remember, nature journaling is a personal and creative practice. There are no right or wrong ways to do it. Let your journaling process be guided by your own observations, feelings, and experiences. Allow yourself to fully embrace the present moment and the beauty of the natural world around you.

# Benefits

Nature Journaling is a simple yet powerful practice that involves integrating mindfulness, creativity, and a deep appreciation for the natural world. Through this practice, you can connect more deeply with your environment, awaken your senses, and tap into the profound healing and restorative powers of nature, ultimately benefiting your mental health and overall well-being.

When you engage in Nature Journaling, you're effectively practising mindfulness - a state of being fully present and engaged in the current moment. This act of focusing your attention, engaging your senses, and writing about your observations allows you to anchor yourself in the 'now', reducing the likelihood of your mind wandering off into worries about the future or preoccupations from the past. Research has demonstrated that mindfulness can reduce stress, anxiety, and depression, and enhance overall wellbeing.

Moreover, the act of describing your observations and feelings in a journal serves as a form of self-expression and emotional release. The simple act of putting pen to paper and expressing your thoughts and emotions can have therapeutic effects, helping you to process emotions, increase self-awareness, and gain new perspectives.

When Nature Journaling is done outdoors in a green space, it combines the benefits of mindfulness and journaling with the mental health benefits of spending time in nature. Research has shown that exposure to green spaces can reduce stress, improve mood, enhance cognitive function, and even boost the immune system. The sights, sounds, and smells of nature can have a calming and restorative effect on the mind, contributing to mental clarity and emotional balance.

On top of that, if you decide to sketch or paint as part of your Nature Journaling practice, you engage in another form of mindfulness and self-expression. Artistic activities like these have been shown to induce a state of 'flow', a highly focused mental state that can foster a sense of joy, creativity, and fulfilment.

In conclusion, Nature Journaling is a multi-faceted practice that combines mindfulness, expressive writing, artistic creativity, and ecotherapy, providing numerous benefits for mental health and wellbeing. It serves as an invitation to slow down, appreciate the beauty of the natural world, and tap into your senses and emotions in a profoundly enriching way. This is a practice that encourages you to build a deeper connection with the environment and with your inner self, promoting a sense of peace, joy, and clarity.

# Practice 11: Mindful Walking

Whether it's a designated nature trail or a tree-lined street, turn your walk into a mindfulness practice. Focus on the sensation of your feet touching the ground, the rhythm of your breath, the feel of the breeze against your skin, or the scent of blossoms in the air. By focusing your attention on these sensations, you can anchor yourself in the present moment. Here is a step-by-step guide to begin your mindful walk.

## Instructions

**Step 1: Choose Your Walking Route**
Select a walking route that includes a natural environment, such as a park, nature trail, or tree-lined street. Find a path that allows you to immerse yourself in the beauty of nature while providing a safe and comfortable walking experience.

**Step 2: Set Your Intention**
Before you begin walking, set your intention to practice mindfulness and be fully present in the moment. Remind yourself that this is an opportunity to slow down, connect with nature, and cultivate a sense of inner calm.

### Step 3: Start with a Mindful Pause

Take a moment to stand still at the beginning of your walk. Close your eyes or soften your gaze and take a few deep breaths. Allow yourself to become aware of your body, the environment, and the present moment.

### Step 4: Engage Your Senses

As you start walking, bring your attention to your senses. Notice the sensation of your feet touching the ground with each step. Pay attention to the movement of your body and the flow of your breath. Observe the sights, sounds, smells, and even the tastes around you. Engage all your senses to fully immerse yourself in the present experience.

### Step 5: Stay Focused on the Present Moment

Instead of letting your mind wander to past or future thoughts, gently bring your attention back to the present moment. If you notice your mind drifting, simply acknowledge it without judgment and redirect your focus to your senses and the act of walking.

### Step 6: Tune into Your Body

Throughout your walk, tune into the sensations in your body. Notice the movement of your legs, the swing of your arms, and the alignment of your posture. Pay attention to any physical sensations or areas of tension or relaxation.

Allow your body to guide your awareness and bring you into the present moment.

**Step 7: Appreciate Nature's Beauty**

Take the time to observe and appreciate the natural environment around you. Notice the colours, shapes, and textures of the plants, trees, flowers, or natural elements you encounter. Listen to the sounds of birds, wind rustling through the leaves, or the flowing of water if available. Take in the scents of the air and feel the temperature and breeze against your skin. Allow yourself to fully connect with the beauty of nature.

**Step 8: Walk at a Comfortable Pace**

Walk at a pace that feels natural and comfortable for you. There is no need to rush or push yourself. Allow your body to set the rhythm, and be mindful of the sensations with each step you take.

**Step 9: Practice Non-Judgmental Awareness**

As you walk, maintain an attitude of non-judgmental awareness. Avoid labelling experiences as good or bad, pleasant or unpleasant. Simply observe and accept whatever arises without attaching any judgments or expectations.

### Step 10 Conclude with Gratitude

When you reach the end of your walk, take a moment to express gratitude for the opportunity to be in nature and engage in this mindful practice. Reflect on any insights, feelings, or moments of peace that you experienced during the walk.

Remember, the practice of mindful walking is about being fully present in the moment and connecting with nature. Allow yourself to let go of distractions and immerse yourself in the experience of walking and the beauty of the natural world around you.

# Benefits

Mindful Walking is a form of meditation where mindfulness is practiced while walking, particularly in a natural setting. This practice can be particularly beneficial for individuals who find it challenging to sit still during meditation. By integrating mindfulness into a physical activity like walking, one can achieve a state of focused attention and heightened awareness, fostering a greater sense of peace, balance, and connectedness with the natural world.

Mindful Walking offers the benefits of traditional

mindfulness meditation, including stress reduction, improved focus, and enhanced mental wellbeing. By paying close attention to the physical sensations of walking, such as the feel of the ground under your feet, the rhythm of your breath, or the swing of your arms, you can help anchor your awareness in the present moment. This can quiet the mind, reduce stress, and help you gain a deeper appreciation for the simple act of moving your body.

In addition to this, Mindful Walking in a natural setting can offer the added benefits of nature therapy. Multiple studies have shown that spending time in nature can reduce feelings of stress, anxiety, and depression, boost mood, and improve overall mental health. The sights, sounds, and smells of nature can have a soothing effect, and the physical activity itself can release endorphins, the body's natural mood elevators.

Engaging your senses in a mindful way during your walk - such as noticing the scent of flowers, the sound of birds, and the feel of the breeze - can enhance your sense of connectedness with the natural world. This can foster feelings of awe and gratitude, which have been linked to improved well-being and happiness.

Furthermore, Mindful Walking can be a gentle form of exercise, promoting cardiovascular health, improving physical strength and flexibility, and boosting energy levels. Regular physical activity, particularly in green spaces, has been linked to improved physical health and longevity.

To conclude, Mindful Walking is a powerful practice that combines the benefits of mindfulness meditation, nature therapy, and physical activity. It is a simple, accessible way to enhance your physical and mental well-being, promote a sense of inner peace, and foster a deeper appreciation for the natural world. Whether you're strolling through a park, hiking in the woods, or simply walking down a tree-lined street, integrating mindfulness into your walk can transform an ordinary activity into a profound, nourishing experience.

# Practice 12: Sound Mapping

In a green space, sit with your eyes closed and listen to all the sounds around you. Try to identify as many different sounds as you can - perhaps the rustling of leaves, a distant car horn, a bird singing, children laughing. This practice can help to quiet the mind and bring a sense of peace and calm.

# Instructions

### Step 1: Find a Quiet Spot

Choose a quiet spot in a green space where you can sit comfortably. It could be a park, a garden, or any other natural area where you can relax without distractions.

### Step 2: Close Your Eyes and Focus

Close your eyes to eliminate visual distractions and bring your attention inward. Take a few deep breaths to centre yourself and prepare for the practice.

### Step 3: Listen to the Sounds

As you sit with your eyes closed, focus your attention on the sounds around you. Try to tune in to the subtle and distant sounds as well as the more prominent ones. Be open and receptive to the variety of sounds that you encounter.

### Step 4: Identify Different Sounds

As you listen, try to identify and mentally note as many different sounds as possible. Pay attention to the rustling of leaves, the chirping of birds, the wind blowing through the trees, the buzzing of insects, or any other sounds that you can discern. Take your time and allow yourself to fully immerse in the auditory experience.

### Step 5: Observe Without Judgment

As you identify each sound, practice observing them without judgment or interpretation. Allow the sounds to come and go without getting caught up in any particular sound or attaching meaning to them. Simply be present and aware of the sounds as they arise and fade away.

### Step 6: Create a Mental Map

As you identify each sound, you can create a mental map or visualisation of the different sources of sound around you. Picture the locations of the sounds in your mind, imagining the distance and direction from where they are coming.

### Step 7: Embrace the Silence

In between the sounds, notice the moments of silence. Embrace these moments and allow them to deepen your sense of calm and presence. Silence can be just as powerful as sound in cultivating mindfulness.

**Step 8: Reflect on the Experience**

After spending some time listening to the sounds, gently bring your awareness back to your surroundings. Take a moment to reflect on the experience. Notice any shifts in your state of mind, any emotions or sensations that arose, and any sense of connection or peace that you may have experienced.

**Step 9: Express Gratitude**

Before concluding the practice, express gratitude for the opportunity to listen and connect with the sounds of nature. Acknowledge the richness and diversity of the natural soundscape and appreciate the peace and tranquillity it brings.

Remember, the practice of Sound Mapping is about cultivating deep listening and awareness of the sounds in the present moment. By immersing yourself in the sounds of nature, you can enhance your mindfulness and find moments of calm and connection.

# Benefits

Sound Mapping is a mindfulness practice that brings us into a unique, sensory interaction with the natural world. This practice involves deep immersion in the auditory experiences offered by our environment, from the rustling of leaves to distant bird songs, creating a rich tapestry of sounds that can soothe and revitalise our minds.

Cultivating mindfulness through Sound Mapping can have profound impacts on mental health. By focusing attention on the natural sounds around us, we ground ourselves in the present moment, quietening the mind from the usual chatter of our thoughts. This immersion in 'here' and 'now' can offer a sense of peace and tranquillity that reduces stress and anxiety. Over time, this training in mindfulness helps enhance our ability to regulate our emotions, resulting in more balanced emotional states, and thus, improved mood.

Moreover, Sound Mapping deepens our connection with nature. As we map the sounds in our surroundings, we become more aware of the world outside our personal sphere. This heightened awareness fosters a greater sense of belonging to the natural world. Research has consistently shown that strengthening our connection with nature can lead to significant improvements in well-being, creating a sense of calm and contentment that permeates our daily lives.

The process of identifying and locating sounds also exercises our cognitive abilities. It involves spatial reasoning, memory, and attention, which are all enhanced during this process. These cognitive benefits can extend beyond the practice, improving mental agility and focus in other areas of life.

Despite the hustle and bustle of our everyday lives, Sound Mapping encourages us to slow down and embrace the silence in between the sounds. These moments of silence are powerful, providing us with an opportunity to just 'be'. This acceptance and embrace of silence can further deepen the sense of calm and peace, promoting relaxation and potentially improving sleep quality.

Lastly, engaging in Sound Mapping often leaves us with a sense of gratitude and appreciation. The realisation of the richness and diversity of the natural soundscape around us can evoke feelings of awe and wonder, enhancing our overall life satisfaction. This sense of gratitude is a powerful boost to our mood and overall mental well-being.

To summarise, Sound Mapping provides a multi-faceted approach to enhancing mental health and well-being. From reducing stress and anxiety to boosting cognitive abilities, fostering a connection with nature, and evoking a sense of gratitude, this simple yet powerful practice has much to offer. Without the need for any technology, it's an accessible way for anyone to cultivate mindfulness and enjoy the therapeutic benefits of connecting with the natural world.

# Practice 13: Nature Mindfulness Scavenger Hunt

Create a list of natural elements or features that can be found in your local urban environment, such as different types of leaves, flowers, rocks, or bird species. Take a walk in a nearby park or green space and challenge yourself to find and observe each item on the list. This activity encourages you to engage with the present moment, sharpen your senses, and deepen your connection with nature.

# Instructions

### Step 1: Create a Nature Scavenger Hunt List

Make a list of natural elements or features that can be found in your local urban environment. These can include different types of leaves, flowers, rocks, bird species, or any other natural objects that are common in your area. Be creative and tailor the list to your surroundings.

### Step 2: Grab a Notebook and Pen

Bring along a notebook or a piece of paper and a pen to record your findings during the scavenger hunt.

### Step 3: Visit a Local Park or Green Space

Choose a nearby park or green space where you can embark

on your nature scavenger hunt. Ensure that it is an area where you are allowed to explore and collect items if necessary.

## Step 4: Review the Scavenger Hunt List
Take a moment to review the scavenger hunt list you created. Familiarise yourself with the items you need to find and observe during your walk.

## Step 5: Start the Scavenger Hunt
Begin your walk in the park or green space, keeping your eyes open for the items on your list. Take your time to observe your surroundings and look for the specific natural elements you are searching for. Use your senses to engage with the environment - feel the textures, smell the scents, and listen to the sounds of nature.

## Step 6: Document your Findings
As you discover each item on the scavenger hunt list, document your findings in your notebook. You can draw sketches, write descriptions, or take photographs of the items you encounter. Take a moment to appreciate the beauty and uniqueness of each element you find.

## Step 7: Stay Mindful and Present
Throughout the scavenger hunt, practice mindfulness by

staying fully present and engaged with the experience. Notice the details, colours, and patterns of the natural elements you discover. Use all your senses to immerse yourself in the present moment.

### Step 8: Reflect on your Experience

After completing the scavenger hunt, find a quiet spot in the park or green space to sit and reflect on your experience. Take a few moments to contemplate the connections you felt with nature, the new discoveries you made, and the overall sense of presence and mindfulness that the activity brought.

### Step 9: Express Gratitude

Before leaving the park or green space, take a moment to express gratitude for the opportunity to engage with nature and experience mindfulness. Appreciate the natural world and its ability to provide peace, inspiration, and a sense of connection.

The Nature Mindfulness Scavenger Hunt combines the excitement of a scavenger hunt with the practice of mindfulness and connection with nature. It encourages you to slow down, observe your surroundings, and appreciate the beauty and wonders of the natural environment in your urban area. Enjoy the process of discovery and the sense of mindfulness it brings.

# Benefits

The practice of Nature Mindfulness Scavenger Hunt provides a dynamic and engaging way to enhance mental health and well-being. This activity combines the intrigue of a scavenger hunt with the peace and tranquillity of being in nature, and the resulting blend fosters a unique synergy that supports psychological health.

The act of creating a list of natural elements to find in an urban environment requires focus, which can be a beneficial cognitive exercise in and of itself. Searching for these elements encourages awareness of the present moment, a cornerstone of mindfulness. Such mindful awareness has been linked to reduced levels of stress and anxiety and increased emotional regulation, fostering a more balanced and calm mental state.

Moreover, the process of focusing our senses on the natural elements around us can be particularly grounding. It helps anchor us in the present moment, quieting the mind from its usual stream of thoughts and concerns. In these moments, we are allowing our minds to rest, which can be rejuvenating and can lead to enhanced clarity and focus even after the activity ends.

On a deeper level, the scavenger hunt can foster a greater connection to nature. By identifying and observing various elements of nature closely, we're encouraged to appreciate the intricacies and beauty of the natural world. This sense of connection and belonging to nature has been shown to boost psychological well-being and elicit feelings of happiness and contentment.

This practice also instigates curiosity and a sense of discovery, which can stimulate a positive mood. It encourages a shift from a passive to an active engagement with our environment. This active involvement can lead to feelings of accomplishment and satisfaction, boosting self-esteem and overall happiness.

Lastly, documenting findings, whether through drawing, writing, or photography, allows for a moment of reflection and appreciation. It can stimulate creativity and provide a tangible reminder of the experience, prolonging the psychological benefits beyond the duration of the activity itself.

In summary, the Nature Mindfulness Scavenger Hunt offers a multitude of benefits for mental health and well-being. It is a practice that fosters mindfulness, encourages active engagement with the environment, stimulates creativity, deepens our connection with nature, and ultimately, serves as a powerful tool to enhance emotional well-being and psychological resilience.

# Practice 14: Barefoot Park Walks

If it's safe, consider walking barefoot on grass or sand in local parks. This practice, known as grounding or earthing, allows for a direct physical connection with the earth and has been found to offer various health benefits. Barefoot walks or "earthing" can be a relaxing and enjoyable way to reconnect with nature. Here's a guide on how to safely and mindfully practice this activity.

## Instructions

### Step 1: Choose a Suitable Location

Find a local park, beach, or grassy area where it's safe and comfortable to walk barefoot. Look for a clean, well-maintained space. Avoid areas with lots of litter, sharp rocks, or broken glass.

### Step 2: Prepare Yourself

Make sure your feet are clean and free from cuts or open wounds. If you're not used to walking barefoot outdoors, you might want to start slowly. Perhaps begin by standing barefoot on the grass, gradually increasing your walking time.

## Step 3: Walk Mindfully

Remove your shoes and socks, then step onto the grass or sand. Pay attention to the sensation of the earth beneath your feet. How does the texture feel against your skin? Is the ground warm or cool? Soft or hard? Feel the connection between your body and the earth. Try to stay present and conscious of your surroundings.

## Step 4: Be Aware of Your Steps

Watch your step as you walk. Pay attention to how your foot moves, how your weight shifts from one foot to the other, and the different sensations you feel with each step. Be aware of your pace - try not to rush, but walk slowly and deliberately.

## Step 5: Connect with Your Surroundings

As you walk, take the time to observe your surroundings. Listen to the sounds of nature, take deep breaths of fresh air, and appreciate the beauty around you. This practice is not just about walking barefoot - it's about immersing yourself in nature and reconnecting with the earth.

## Step 6: Reflect

After your walk, sit for a while and reflect on your experience. How do you feel? More relaxed? Energized? Paying attention to these feelings can help deepen your connection to nature and the practice of barefoot walking.

**Step 7: Clean Up**

After your walk, make sure to clean your feet properly. You can bring a small towel or wet wipes for this purpose if you're far from home.

Walking barefoot in nature can be a therapeutic and grounding practice that promotes a deeper sense of connection with the earth. As with any new activity, it's important to start slow, pay attention to your body's responses, and, most importantly, enjoy the experience.

# Benefits

Engaging in barefoot park walks can offer numerous benefits to a person's mental health and well-being. The act of walking barefoot in nature allows for a direct physical connection with the earth, providing a unique and grounding experience. This practice, often referred to as "earthing" or "grounding," can have a profound impact on our overall well-being.

One of the primary benefits of barefoot park walks is the opportunity to reconnect with nature. In our fast-paced, technology-driven world, it's easy to feel disconnected from the natural environment. Walking barefoot in a park provides an opportunity to immerse ourselves in the sights, sounds, and sensations of nature. The feeling of grass or sand beneath our feet, the gentle breeze on our skin, and the scent of the outdoors can awaken our senses and bring a sense of peace and tranquillity.

Moreover, barefoot park walks encourage mindfulness and present-moment awareness. As we focus on the sensation of the earth beneath our feet, we naturally become more attuned to the present moment. The rhythmic act of walking, combined with the direct connection to nature, can help quiet the mind and bring a sense of calm. This mindful presence allows us to let go of worries, stresses, and distractions and instead fully embrace the experience of the present moment.

Engaging in barefoot park walks can also foster a sense of connection and belonging. When we walk barefoot, we become part of the natural world around us. We acknowledge our interconnectedness with the earth, the plants, and the creatures that inhabit these spaces. This recognition of our place in the larger web of life can cultivate feelings of gratitude, humility, and a deeper sense of purpose.

Additionally, barefoot park walks promote physical well-being. Walking barefoot stimulates the nerve endings in our feet, which can enhance balance, proprioception, and foot strength. It encourages a more natural and grounded way of moving as we adapt to the changing textures and contours of the ground. The gentle exercise of walking can also contribute to increased circulation, improved cardiovascular health, and overall physical vitality.

In summary, engaging in barefoot park walks provides a range of benefits to a person's mental health and well-being. It reconnects us with nature, cultivates mindfulness, fosters a sense of connection and belonging, and promotes physical well-being. By embracing this simple yet powerful practice, we can find solace, rejuvenation, and a deeper appreciation for the natural world that surrounds us.

# Reflections on Cultivating Wholeness, Connecting to Spirit & Embracing Awe

In today's fast-paced, tech-saturated world, many of us feel fragmented, longing for a sense of wholeness that seems elusive. But the secret might just lie in our ancient roots: Nature.

Nature isn't just a destination; it's a wellspring of spirit, awe, and wholeness. Within its embrace, our frazzled souls find peace and rejuvenation. It reminds us of the awe-inspiring wonder of the universe and our precious place within it. This wonder, described as "awe", is a deep emotion we feel in the presence of vast and incomprehensible beauty. It has the power to diminish our egos and fill us with a sense of belonging[113].

When we dive into nature's embrace, we're not just taking in the sights; we're connecting with a force larger than ourselves, fostering a spirit of unity with our surroundings[137]. This sense of unity goes beyond mere relaxation. It aligns us with an ancient understanding of the world, one where spirit isn't confined to religious dogma, but rather, found in the whisper of leaves, the dance of fireflies, and the vastness of the night sky[138].

Centuries-old indigenous teachings, like those of the Native American traditions, have long recognised this connection. They teach that our spirit thrives when we walk harmoniously with nature, emphasising a bond between mind, body, spirit, and the environment. Such wisdom encourages us to value and respect all life forms, guiding us towards a profound feeling of interconnectedness.

By truly immersing ourselves in nature, even within the city's heart, we nurture a value system that cherishes every living thing. We become more mindful, present, and attuned to our innate connection with the environment. Such experiences open doors to profound moments where we don't just see nature but feel deeply intertwined with it[139].

Yes, our world has transformed, often prioritising progress over the environment, leading to a feeling of disconnection[140]. Yet, the natural antidote remains the same. Reconnecting with nature can rekindle our sense of spirit, wholeness, and awe. It can help heal our mental and emotional scars, inspiring us to lead lives that resonate with meaning, harmony, and joy.

In the grand tapestry of life, our pursuit of wholeness is deeply tied to nature. The urban jungle might seem distant from the forests of old, but the spirit of nature is ever-present, waiting to guide us back to a state of awe, connection, and profound wholeness. Let us now delve into our final series of practices. My hope is that these practices open your heart to wholeness, spirit and moments of awe.

# Practice 15: Forest Bathing in the City

While the term originated in Japan, known as Shinrin-yoku, the concept can be adapted to urban settings by visiting local parks or green spaces. Spend time simply being in nature, absorbing the atmosphere through all your senses. Take deep breaths, listen to the rustling leaves or chirping birds, touch the bark of trees, and notice the various shades of green around you. Here is a step-by-step guide to forest bathing in an urban setting.

## Instructions

**Step 1: Choose Your Forest**

In an urban environment, a forest may not always be readily available. That's okay - any green space can work for this exercise. This could be a park, a community garden, a greenway, or even a tree-lined street. Wherever you choose, make sure it's a place where you feel safe and can relax.

**Step 2: Set Aside Time**

Ensure you have enough uninterrupted time for your forest bathing experience. While there is no prescribed duration, aim for at least 20-30 minutes, though longer is welcome if you can manage. The key is to allow yourself plenty of time to slow down and connect with the natural environment without feeling rushed.

## Step 3: Leave Your Devices Behind

If possible, try to leave behind your phone or any other device that may be distracting. The aim is to connect with nature, not technology.

## Step 4: Enter the Space Mindfully

As you enter your chosen green space, take a moment to consciously acknowledge your transition from the urban environment into nature. Breathe deeply, relax your body, and open your senses.

## Step 5: Slow Down

Start walking slowly, taking time to observe your surroundings. Try not to have a destination in mind, but instead, allow yourself to be drawn towards whatever captures your attention.

## Step 6: Engage Your Senses

Take in the sights around you - the different shades of green, the way the sunlight filters through the leaves, the shapes of trees and plants. Listen to the sounds - bird calls, rustling leaves, the wind. Feel the texture of tree bark or the smoothness of a leaf. If it's safe and non-destructive, taste berries or edible leaves. Smell the fresh, earthy scent of the greenery or the perfume of flowers. The goal is to fully immerse yourself in the sensory experiences that the natural environment offers.

### Step 7: Sit or Lie Down

If it feels right, find a spot to sit or lie down. This could be under a tree or on a patch of soft grass. Continue engaging your senses as you stay stationary, observing the world around you from a different perspective.

### Step 8: Reflect

Towards the end of your forest bathing session, take a few moments to reflect on your experience. What did you notice? How do you feel? What impact has the experience had on your well-being or state of mind?

### Step 9: Gradually Return

As you leave the green space, transition gently back into the urban environment. Carry the sense of calm and connectedness with you as you re-enter the bustle of city life.

Remember, there is no right or wrong way to practice forest bathing. It's about being present and developing a personal connection with nature, experiencing it fully with all your senses. It's a unique journey for each person. Enjoy your forest bathing experience!

# Benefits

As noted earlier, Forest Bathing, known in Japan as Shinrin-yoku, has been steadily gaining recognition worldwide due to its impressive ability to boost mental health and foster overall well-being, even when adapted for urban settings. At its core, this practice encourages us to be present in nature and absorb its calming and rejuvenating effects through all of our senses.

The immersion in nature, even within the bounds of a city, presents a form of therapy that caters to our intrinsic need to connect with the natural world. This connection can instil a profound sense of peace and tranquillity, serving as a powerful antidote to the hustle and bustle of city life. This peaceful state of mind can significantly reduce stress levels, improve mood, and enhance overall emotional health.

Mindfulness plays a central role in Forest Bathing. As we engage our senses fully to appreciate the rustling leaves, the scent of damp earth, the varying hues of greenery, or the song of a distant bird, we anchor ourselves in the present moment. This practice of being fully present helps quiet the mind, warding off anxiety and depressive thoughts. Research has shown that mindfulness practices can improve cognitive abilities, boost creativity, and enhance emotional regulation.

Taking deep, intentional breaths as part of this

practice serves to further accentuate its calming effect. Deep breathing has been shown to reduce the body's stress response and promote relaxation, leading to improved mental clarity and focus.

In addition, the act of physically touching elements of nature, such as tree bark or leaves, adds a tactile dimension to the experience, further strengthening our sense of connection to the natural world. This engagement can stimulate a sense of joy, curiosity, and wonder, revitalising our mental state and serving as a natural mood booster.

Reflecting on the experience after a session of Forest Bathing can lead to greater self-awareness and foster a deeper understanding of our relationship with nature. This introspection can lead to personal growth, an increased sense of purpose, and an enhanced appreciation for the natural world.

Finally, the practice of Forest Bathing reinforces our sense of being part of a larger whole, which can combat feelings of isolation or disconnection. This increased feeling of connectivity fosters a sense of belonging and improves our overall well-being.

In essence, Forest Bathing in the city presents a viable, technology-free strategy to improve mental health and well-being. It highlights nature's ability to heal and restore, helping us find peace, joy, and connection amidst our busy urban lives.

*I have two routes to the city centre: one is by taking the road that leads to the town centre, and the other is through this beautiful tree line at the back of my apartment.*

*Naturally, I choose the latter.*

# Practice 16: Lunchtime Picnics

Rather than eating at your desk or in a city café, take your lunch to a local park or green space. This simple practice allows you to slow down, appreciate your surroundings, and cultivate gratitude for nature, even amidst a busy day. Here is a step-by-step guide.

# Instructions

### Step 1: Prepare Your Lunch
Pack your lunch in reusable containers, being mindful of choosing items that are easy to eat outdoors. Remember to bring a beverage to stay hydrated.

### Step 2: Choose a Location
Identify a green space in your area where you can have your lunch. This could be a park, a bench under a tree, or even a rooftop garden. Choose a location that is easily accessible from your place of work or home, and that offers a space to sit and relax.

### Step 3: Bring a Blanket or Mat
If you're planning to sit on the grass, bring along a blanket or a picnic mat. This will keep you comfortable and help

create a distinct space for your picnic.

**Step 4: Disconnect from Technology**

If possible, leave your phone or other electronic devices behind, or at least set them aside. The goal is to take a break from screens and fully engage with the experience.

**Step 5: Make Your Way to the Location Mindfully**

As you walk to your picnic spot, pay attention to your surroundings. Notice the play of light and shadow, the colour of the leaves, the sounds of the city. Use this time to transition from work mode to relaxation mode.

**Step 6: Set Up Your Picnic Spot**

Spread out your blanket or mat and arrange your food. Take a moment to appreciate the effort you've put into preparing your lunch and setting up your picnic.

**Step 7: Eat Mindfully**

As you eat, pay attention to the flavours and textures of your food. Try to eat slowly, savouring each bite. This mindful eating practice can enhance your enjoyment of the meal and create a deeper sense of connection with the food you're consuming.

**Step 8: Engage with Nature**

While you're eating or after you finish, take the time to observe the nature around you. Watch the birds, admire the trees, and feel the grass under your hands. Let your senses fully engage with the environment.

**Step 9: Clean Up**

Once you've finished eating, ensure you leave no trace behind. Pack up any waste and dispose of it properly.

**Step 10: Return to Your Routine**

As you head back to your daily routine, try to carry the sense of peace and connection you gained during your lunchtime picnic. Use it as a source of energy and inspiration for the rest of your day.

Remember, the goal of this practice is not only to have lunch, but to create a meaningful connection with nature that can enhance your well-being and provide a refreshing break from your everyday routine. Enjoy your lunchtime picnic!

# Benefits

A seemingly simple act, the transition from consuming lunch within the confines of your workspace or a bustling city café to the peaceful embrace of a local park or green space, can have profound effects on mental health and well-being. This practice is not just about the physical act of eating; it's a holistic experience designed to recharge the mind and nourish the soul.

In our fast-paced urban lives, we're often wrapped up in an endless loop of tasks and responsibilities. Taking your lunch outdoors offers an invitation to slow down and disconnect from this whirlwind of activity. It's a slice of 'me-time' nestled into your day, a pause button that allows you to relax and catch your breath amidst a busy schedule. By creating a physical and mental distance from the workspace it allows stress levels to decrease, improving mood and productivity for the rest of the day.

This practice also paves the way for mindfulness. Mindful eating, an integral part of the picnic experience, involves savouring each bite, acknowledging the taste, texture, and aroma of the food, and truly appreciating the meal. This not only enhances the dining experience but also improves digestion, contributes to better nutrition, and creates a more intimate relationship with our food.

Furthermore, the act of preparing your picnic lunch can instil a sense of accomplishment and self-care, reminding us that we are deserving of our own time and effort. It encourages healthier food choices, influencing physical health, which is inextricably linked with mental well-being.

Immersing ourselves in green spaces for our lunchtime break allows for a connection with nature that we often lack in urban settings. It's a moment to soak in the sights, sounds, and smells of the natural world. This sensory engagement grounds us in the present, promotes mindfulness and fosters a sense of belonging with the natural world. Studies have shown that exposure to nature can lower blood pressure, improve immune function, increase self-esteem, and improve mood, emphasising the importance of this connection.

Finally, as we wrap up our picnic, there's an element of reflection and gratitude. It's an opportunity to appreciate the tranquillity of the environment, the nourishment provided by the meal, and the experience as a whole. This expression of gratitude is a powerful positivity booster and has been linked to increased happiness, reduced depression, and overall improved mental health.

In essence, the practice of a lunchtime picnic in the city is an amalgamation of small steps towards improved mental health and well-being. Each element of the experience, from preparation to consumption to reflection, contributes to creating a healthier, happier mind. This simple yet profound activity serves as a reminder that in the pursuit of well-being, sometimes, all we need is a patch of green, a delicious meal, and a moment of quiet in the sunshine.

# Practice 17: Nature Meditation

Find a quiet spot in a park or garden where you can sit undisturbed. Focus on the sounds, smells, and sensations around you, allowing them to anchor you in the present moment. Notice the sensation of the breeze, the sound of birdsong, the smell of the earth - this practice can help cultivate a sense of peace and a deep connection to the natural world. Here is a step-by-step guide.

# Instructions

### Step 1: Find Your Space

Search for a quiet spot in an urban green space, such as a park, community garden, or even a secluded area within a tree-lined street. Choose a location where you feel safe and can be relatively undisturbed for the duration of your meditation.

### Step 2: Set a Time Limit

If you're new to meditation, start with just a few minutes and gradually increase the duration over time. Even a short practice can be beneficial.

### Step 3: Get Comfortable

Find a comfortable way to sit, whether that's on a bench, a

blanket on the grass, or leaning against a tree. Your comfort is crucial to maintaining focus during the meditation.

## Step 4: Close Your Eyes or Soften Your Gaze

Close your eyes if it feels comfortable, or you can also keep them open with a soft gaze directed downwards or towards nature around you.

## Step 5: Draw Attention to Your Breath

Notice the flow of your breath, the rise and fall of your chest or abdomen. This will help anchor your mind and keep it from wandering.

## Step 6: Engage Your Senses

Once you're settled, bring awareness to your senses. Notice the sounds around you - perhaps the rustling of leaves or distant city noises. Pay attention to the scents that the wind brings - the smell of trees, flowers, or grass. Feel the temperature of the air and the sensations of the ground beneath you. Open yourself to the whole sensory experience.

## Step 7: Acknowledge Your Thoughts

If thoughts arise during your meditation, which they often do, simply acknowledge them without judgment and let them pass, gently returning your focus to your senses.

### Step 8: Cultivate Gratitude

Towards the end of your meditation, spend a moment acknowledging the beauty of nature around you. Cultivate a sense of gratitude for these moments of peace amidst your city life.

### Step 9: Gently Wrap Up

When you're ready to end your meditation, bring your attention back to your breath. Gradually move your fingers and toes, slowly open your eyes (if they were closed), and take a moment to transition out of the meditation.

Remember, there's no right or wrong way to meditate. The purpose of this practice is to bring you into a deeper connection with the present moment and the natural world around you, even within the urban bustle. Enjoy your nature meditation!

# Benefits

Engaging in nature meditation is a remarkable journey that combines the profound tranquillity of natural environments with the grounding practice of meditation. It is an activity that transcends the simple action of being still, creating a holistic experience that nourishes both mind and body.

In the heart of the city, where the hustle and bustle

can feel overwhelming, finding a quiet spot within a park or garden is akin to finding an oasis. The natural setting becomes a sanctuary, providing a respite from the constant stimuli of urban life. This shift in environment encourages a sense of peace and relaxation, which is the first step towards effective meditation.

Focusing on the sensory experience of the natural world is the cornerstone of nature meditation. By directing your attention to the sounds, smells, and sensations around you, your mind gradually detaches from the anxieties and preoccupations of daily life. The melody of birdsong, the fragrance of the earth, the gentle caress of the breeze - these experiences anchor you firmly in the present moment. Mindfulness experts suggest that this practice enhances awareness and promotes a serene mental state.

Moreover, this form of meditation fosters a deep connection with the natural world. In urban settings, it is easy to feel disconnected from nature, an experience that can lead to feelings of isolation or stress. By immersing yourself in the natural elements of the city, you are reminded of the intricate web of life to which you belong, cultivating feelings of unity and belonging.

The practice of nature meditation is also a pathway to developing gratitude. Amid the high-speed rhythms of city life, it's easy to overlook the beauty and serenity that nature provides. Yet, by engaging with the sensory experiences of the natural world in a mindful way, you become more appreciative of these gifts. Gratitude itself is strongly associated with increased happiness and improved mental health, reinforcing the benefits of the practice.

In essence, the practice of nature meditation is more than a mere break from city life. It is an exercise in mindfulness, an invitation to connect with the natural world, and a practice of gratitude. The convergence of these elements within the meditative experience can contribute significantly to mental well-being, providing a calming refuge in the heart of the city.

*The practice of 'Nature Meditation' has deeply enriched my life, serving as a bridge that not only connects me intimately with the natural world but also reacquaints me with the profound inner stillness that we, as beings of this Earth, inherently possess but often lose touch with in the clamour of modern life.*

# Practice 18: Cloud Watching

This is a practice as old as time. Find a grassy spot in your nearest park, lie back, and observe the clouds. Try to do this mindfully, watching the shapes shift and change, noting the colours and light, and feeling the sensation of the earth beneath you. This simple practice encourages slowing down, imaginative thinking, and deepening your connection with nature. Here is a step-by-step guide to get the most out of your cloud watching experience.

# Instructions

### Step 1: Find Your Spot

Locate a green space in your vicinity - it could be a park, a community garden, or even a secluded, grassy area in your apartment complex. It should be a place where you can lie down and comfortably observe the sky.

### Step 2: Choose the Right Time

Cloud watching can be done at any time of the day, but you may find it particularly enjoyable on a day when the sky is filled with fluffy clouds, or as the sun is setting and colors are more vibrant.

## Step 3: Get Comfortable

Bring along a blanket or a mat to lie on. Lie down on your back and adjust your position until you're comfortable. You could also prop your head up with your backpack or a rolled-up jacket.

## Step 4: Look Up

Turn your gaze towards the sky. Let your eyes relax and don't focus too hard on anything in particular. Allow the clouds to enter your field of vision naturally.

## Step 5: Be Mindful

Try to bring your full attention to the process of cloud watching. Observe the shapes, colours, and patterns that the clouds form. Notice how they change and move across the sky. Be present in the moment without thinking about the past or future.

## Step 6: Use Your Imagination

Allow your imagination to play with the shapes and forms of the clouds. Do you see animals, faces, or fantastical creatures? This exercise can stimulate creativity and bring a sense of childlike wonder.

## Step 7: Engage Your Other Senses

While your primary focus is on the clouds, try to also engage your other senses. Notice the feel of the grass beneath you, the smell of the earth, the sound of the wind rustling the trees or birds chirping.

**Step 8: Embrace Tranquillity**
Cloud watching can be a very peaceful experience. Embrace this tranquillity and let it soothe your mind. Even in the middle of a bustling city, these quiet moments can be deeply restorative.

**Step 9: Return Gradually**
After cloud watching, sit up slowly and give yourself a few moments to transition back to the pace of everyday life. Bring this sense of calm and wonder with you as you go about your day.

Remember, the goal of cloud watching isn't to accomplish anything. It's about taking time to slow down, reconnect with nature, and simply be present. Enjoy this serene practice!

# Benefits

Immersing oneself in the age-old practice of cloud watching is a soothing journey into the world of mindful observation and imaginative thought. This practice not only encourages mental wellbeing but also kindles our inherent connectivity with nature. Here is a deeper dive into the essence of this practice.

Within the heart of the urban landscape, a green spot under the open sky becomes a perfect sanctuary for a session of cloud watching. Be it a park, a common green area, or a private garden, these spaces offer a slice of nature where one can lay back and gaze upwards into the vastness of the sky.

Timing can greatly enhance the cloud watching experience. A sky filled with fluffy, billowing clouds or the changing hues at dusk provides a fascinating spectacle for the watcher. However, the beauty of this practice lies in its flexibility. It can be done at any time when the sky is visible, turning the most mundane of days into an opportunity for mindful engagement with nature.

The next step is to ensure comfort. Laying down on a blanket or mat and getting comfortable is crucial. Once you're settled, turn your attention skyward. The infinite canvas of the sky and its shifting tableaux of clouds become the focus.

The mindfulness aspect of cloud watching is deeply entwined with the simple act of observation. The swirling shapes and altering hues, the movement of the clouds against the backdrop of the sky, all demand a focus on the present moment. There's no room for dwelling on the past or anxiety about the future, just an intimate interaction with the ever-changing now.

The clouds also spark the flames of imagination. What figures or stories can you see in their formations? Animals, mythical creatures, or abstract shapes - the possibilities are boundless. This aspect of imaginative thinking adds an extra dimension to the therapeutic value of cloud watching, inspiring creativity and a sense of playful wonder.

The practice extends beyond mere visual engagement. The earth under you, the ambient noises around, the scent carried on the breeze; these sensory experiences enrich the cloud-watching practice, further deepening the connection with nature.

As you indulge in this practice, a tranquillity settles in. Amid the urban chaos, the serene act of cloud watching serves as a mental balm, slowing down the pace of life, even if just for a while. This peaceful interlude can have a profound restorative effect on mental health, instilling a sense of calm that carries forward into the daily routine.

In essence, cloud watching is not an activity with an end goal, but rather an immersive practice that facilitates a slow, mindful engagement with our natural surroundings. It encourages us to pause, to observe, and to dream, threading us back into the tapestry of the natural world around us. This connection, alongside the calm it instils, makes cloud watching a wonderfully beneficial practice for mental well-being in an urban environment.

*I'm sure many of us recall childhood moments, lying on the grass, gazing up at the clouds, and letting our imaginations paint dragons, castles, and countless other wonders in the sky. The beauty of cloud-watching is its universality – it can be enjoyed from any corner of the world. I captured this photo from a bench at Milntown Estate in Ramsey, Isle of Man. The estate spans 15 acres of exquisite gardens and woodlands, all embracing the grand mansion and café at its core.*

# Practice 19: Urban Tree Hugging

This may sound cliché, but taking a moment to embrace a tree can be a surprisingly grounding and healing experience. Touching the bark, feeling the life force within, and appreciating its presence can bring about a deep sense of connection. Here is a step-by-step guide to becoming a 'tree hugger'.

# Instructions

**Step 1: Find Your Tree**

Locate a tree in your local park, street, or even in your backyard if you have one. The tree should be sturdy and healthy. Try to pick one that resonates with you in some way - perhaps it's the shape, size, or just the energy it seems to emanate.

**Step 2: Approach Mindfully**

As you approach the tree, do so with respect and intention. Recognize that you are about to interact with a living organism that shares the same planet as you do.

**Step 3: Make Contact**

Start by gently touching the bark with your hands. Notice the texture, the temperature, and the contours. Then, if you feel comfortable and if it's culturally acceptable where you live, slowly lean into the tree and wrap your arms around it as far as they can reach.

## Step 4: Close Your Eyes

Close your eyes to better focus on the sensation of hugging the tree. Be aware of the solidity and strength of the tree against your body. Feel the earthy smell and the rough texture of the bark.

## Step 5: Tune In

Try to sense the life force of the tree. This can be imagined as a steady, calm energy that the tree has been cultivating for many years, or even decades. Imagine the roots extending deep into the ground, and the branches reaching towards the sky.

## Step 6: Practice Gratitude

Silently thank the tree for its strength and beauty, and for the oxygen it provides. Express gratitude for the shade it gives and the habitat it serves for countless organisms.

## Step 7: Release

When you feel ready, gently release your hug and take a step back. Notice any shifts in your mood or energy levels.

### Step 8: Reflect

Spend a few moments reflecting on the experience. What emotions or thoughts came up during the tree hugging? Can you carry this sense of connection and tranquillity into your daily urban life?

Remember, this practice is less about the physical act of hugging a tree and more about the intention behind it - the desire to connect with nature and acknowledge the living beings that coexist with us in the cityscape. Happy tree-hugging!

# Benefits

As urban environments often distance us from nature, engaging in a practice as simple as hugging a tree can bring us back to a place of groundedness and connection. This practice, though it may sound cliché, has deep roots in holistic well-being, offering a tangible point of contact with the living natural world.

The first step towards tree hugging is to find the right tree. Any urban setting, despite its concrete façade, is dotted with trees — in parks, along streets, or even your backyard. Choosing a tree becomes a personal journey. Each tree resonates differently with each individual. It could be the tree's size, shape, or an inexplicable sense of energy that draws you towards it. Whichever tree you pick, ensure it's sturdy and healthy.

Once you have chosen your tree, the next step is to approach it mindfully. This involves recognizing that you are about to engage with a living entity, a fellow inhabitant of this planet. The act of approaching itself becomes a moment of grounding as you anticipate the contact.

Making contact with the tree is where the physical meets the emotional. As you reach out to touch the tree's bark, notice the texture under your fingertips, the temperature, the unique ridges, and indentations. If you feel comfortable and it's considered appropriate in your culture, gently wrap your arms around the tree, pressing your body lightly against the sturdy trunk.

With your eyes closed, your awareness is pulled towards the contact points between you and the tree. The rough bark against your skin, the solid strength of the trunk, and the scent of earthiness all seep into your consciousness. This sensory immersion enhances your connection with the tree, making the experience deeply personal.

Tuning into the tree's life force is the next part of this practice. Trees, standing tall through seasons and years, carry within them a steady, calm energy. Visualize the roots reaching into the earth's depths for nourishment and the branches spread wide, brushing the sky. This visualization enhances your understanding of the tree's life journey and its interconnectedness with the world around it.

Practicing gratitude towards the tree brings a sense of humility and appreciation. Silently thank the tree for its life-giving oxygen, the shade it provides, and its silent role as a home for countless organisms. This moment of gratitude highlights the often-overlooked contributions of trees to our lives and the ecosystem.

After the hug, it's time to gently pull away. As you step back, carry with you the tranquillity and grounding energy the tree has shared with you. Notice any shift in your mood or energy, any calmness that might have descended, and the renewed sense of connection with nature.

Finally, reflecting on this unique experience allows you to assimilate it into your urban life. Consider the thoughts and emotions that arose during this practice. Ponder how this reconnection with nature could be a source of calm and balance amidst the city's rush.

In essence, urban tree hugging isn't just about the physical act of embracing a tree. It's about recognizing our deep-rooted connection with nature, acknowledging the life around us, and allowing this connection to foster a sense of peace and grounding in our everyday urban existence. Enjoy this profound practice, one hug at a time.

*Just so you know I was being dead serious about the healing power of hugging a tree.*

# Practice 20: Insect Observation

Just like bird watching, observing the world of insects can be fascinating. You can do this in your own garden, a local park, or even an alleyway with plants. Paying attention to these often-overlooked creatures can bring you closer to the intricate interdependencies in nature. Observing insects is a great way to connect with the small but incredibly important aspects of nature that exist even in urban areas.

# Instructions

### Step 1: Find the Right Spot

Begin by finding a spot with plenty of plant life. This could be a public park, a garden, a green strip near a walkway, or even potted plants in your balcony. Anywhere where plants thrive is likely to have an insect population.

### Step 2: Equip Yourself

While no special equipment is necessary for casual observation, a magnifying glass can bring you closer to the world of insects. It's also a good idea to have a notebook and pen to jot down your observations. For identification purposes, an insect guide book or a mobile app could be useful.

**Step 3: Time it Right**

Different insects are active at different times of the day. For instance, many bees and butterflies are most active during the day, while moths and beetles come out at dusk. Be patient and try different times to see a variety of insects.

**Step 4: Observe Quietly**

Approach your chosen spot quietly and make sure not to cast a shadow over the insects, as this may scare them away. Stand or sit still and watch the insects go about their routines. Avoid quick movements which might disturb them.

**Step 5: Pay Attention to Details**

Notice the colours, patterns, and behaviours of the insects you see. How do they interact with each other and with the plants? Do they make any sounds? How do they move? Pay attention to their size, shape, and any distinguishing features.

**Step 6: Sketch or Photograph**

If you're inclined, try sketching the insects you see or taking pictures of them. This can be a great way to remember your observations and share them with others later.

**Step 7: Reflect**

After your observation session, take a moment to reflect on what you've seen. What did you find most fascinating? How did observing insects make you feel? This practice is about fostering a deeper appreciation for all forms of life, no matter how small.

**Step 8: Identify**

Try to identify the insects you've seen using your guidebook or app. Learning more about their habits, life cycles, and roles in the ecosystem can deepen your understanding and appreciation of these tiny creatures.

Remember, the goal is not just to identify insects, but to develop a connection with the often overlooked world of insects and appreciate their crucial role in our ecosystems. Happy insect observing!

# Benefits

In the bustling life of the city, engaging with the often unnoticed world of insects can bring unexpected joys and profound insights. This practice, which we can refer to as Insect Observation, is about noticing the tiny inhabitants of our world, those that quietly contribute to the natural cycle of life around us. It's a form of interaction that takes us away from the everyday hustle and bustle and provides a bridge to the intricate interdependencies in nature.

Just as one might seek the beauty in a sprawling landscape or a sunset, there's beauty to be found in the delicate wings of a butterfly, the methodical work of an ant, or the mesmerizing pattern on a beetle. This isn't a practice that demands an open countryside or vast wilderness; indeed, the world of insects is teeming all around us, even in the most urban environments. An alleyway with plants, a local park, a garden, or simply a tree in the street might be home to a myriad of these small creatures.

Delving into this microscopic world, we come to see the finer details of life that often go unnoticed. Observing these creatures in their natural habitat helps us develop patience, attention to detail, and a sense of awe for life's complexity. We become more aware of our surroundings and begin to appreciate the little things. This, in turn, can instil a sense of tranquillity and focus, benefiting our overall mental well-being.

As we quietly observe, taking care not to disturb the insects in their routines, we connect with nature in a profound, intimate way. We become less detached observers and more active participants in life's rich tapestry, developing a deeper understanding of our place within it. This can lead to a greater sense of belonging and purpose, as well as a newfound respect for all forms of life.

In a world where we're often drawn into the virtual realities created by technology, returning to the physical, tangible world through practices like Insect Observation can be grounding. It reminds us of the richness of experience that the real world offers, an experience that doesn't require a screen or a device, but simply our presence and attention.

Engaging in this practice can be an enriching, restorative activity, enhancing our connection with nature, increasing our attention to detail, fostering patience, and boosting our mental well-being. As we continue to observe, we may find ourselves more present, more aware, and more appreciative of the beauty in the world around us, down to its smallest inhabitants.

*This is a photo I took of a Yellow slug on a wooden railing near my apartment in Douglas, Isle of Man. Though often found in gardens and damp places in homes and sadly considered a pest, this creature plays an important role in nature as a nutrient recycler.*

# Practice 21: Mindful Outdoor Cleaning

Engage in cleaning a local park or green space. This activity not only benefits the community but also encourages a greater sense of responsibility and stewardship for our environment. Mindful outdoor cleaning is a wonderful way to cultivate awareness, care for your community, and foster a connection with nature. Here's a step-by-step guide.

## Instructions

### Step 1: Choose Your Location

Choose a local park, beach, woodland, river bank, or any public green space that could benefit from a clean-up. Make sure to get any necessary permissions from local authorities if needed.

### Step 2: Equip Yourself

You will need a pair of durable gloves, a few trash bags, and possibly a trash picker for this activity. Consider wearing long-sleeved shirts and pants to protect yourself from scrapes or insect bites. If you're cleaning a large area or planning a community event, you may need additional supplies like first-aid kits, water, snacks, and extra gloves and bags.

**Step 3: Set an Intention**

Before you begin, take a moment to set an intention for your activity. This could be as simple as "I am cleaning this park to contribute to my community and care for the environment." Keep this intention in mind throughout the activity.

**Step 4: Clean Mindfully**

As you pick up each piece of litter, do so mindfully. Pay attention to your movements, the feel of the object in your hand, and the sensation of letting it go into the trash bag. Notice any thoughts or emotions that arise without judgment.

**Step 5: Take Breaks**

Remember to take breaks as needed. During these breaks, take the time to appreciate the nature around you. Listen to the birds, feel the breeze, or observe the trees and flowers.

**Step 6: Dispose of the Waste Properly**

After you've finished cleaning, make sure to dispose of the collected waste properly. This could mean taking it home for disposal, or using designated waste disposal facilities in the area.

**Step 7: Reflect on Your Experience**

Once you're done, spend some time reflecting on the

experience. How do you feel about the space now? Do you feel a deeper connection to it? How did the activity affect your mood and mindset?

Remember, the goal of mindful outdoor cleaning is not only to improve your environment but also to foster a deeper connection with nature and the spaces you frequent. This can lead to increased feelings of well-being and a sense of responsibility for your surroundings.

# Benefits

Engaging in mindful outdoor cleaning can have profound benefits for a person's mental health and well-being, fostering a sense of connection, purpose, and responsibility. As you embark on this activity, you enter into a unique opportunity to immerse yourself in the present moment and experience the transformative power of nature.

Cleaning a local park or green space requires your focused attention and intention. As you set out to pick up litter and debris, you become an active participant in improving your environment. This sense of purpose can provide a meaningful boost to your mental well-being, as it gives you a tangible way to contribute to your community and make a positive impact on the world around you.

Mindful outdoor cleaning allows you to develop a deeper connection with nature. By immersing yourself in the process, you become attuned to the sights, sounds, and sensations of the natural environment. The gentle rustling of leaves, the warm touch of sunlight on your skin, and the earthy scents that surround you create a sensory experience that can be deeply calming and grounding. This heightened connection with nature can alleviate stress, reduce anxiety, and promote a sense of peace and tranquillity within.

Engaging in mindful outdoor cleaning also encourages a greater sense of responsibility and stewardship for our environment. By actively participating in the cleaning process, you develop a heightened awareness of the impact of human actions on the natural world. This awareness can translate into a deeper commitment to sustainable living, conservation efforts, and a desire to protect and preserve our planet. Nurturing this sense of responsibility fosters a greater sense of purpose and fulfilment as you align your actions with your values and become an advocate for positive change.

Moreover, engaging in an activity that focuses on cleaning and improving your environment can have a positive effect on your mental clarity and focus. As you direct your attention to the task at hand, you experience a break from the constant stimulation and distractions of daily life. This break allows you to clear your mind, restore mental energy, and improve cognitive function. The act of cleaning becomes a form of meditation, where your mind can find respite and rejuvenation.

Furthermore, mindful outdoor cleaning can foster a sense of community and social connection. It provides an opportunity to engage with like-minded individuals who share a common goal of improving the environment. By participating in cleaning initiatives and joining forces with others, you develop a sense of camaraderie and belonging. Connecting with others who care about the environment can deepen your sense of purpose and create a supportive network of individuals who inspire and motivate one another.

In conclusion, engaging in mindful outdoor cleaning offers a multitude of benefits for a person's mental health and well-being. It allows for a deep connection with nature, promotes a sense of purpose and responsibility, cultivates mental clarity and focus, and fosters social connection. By actively participating in the improvement of your environment, you not only contribute to the well-being of your community but also nurture your own sense of fulfilment, belonging, and connection with the natural world.

# Practice 22: Shadow and Light Observations

Observe how the shadow and light play on natural elements throughout the day. This practice can enhance your perception of the beauty of nature and the passing of time. Observing the interplay of shadow and light is an excellent way to engage with nature. Here's a guide to help you get started with this practice.

# Instructions

### Step 1: Select Your Observation Spot

Firstly, choose a suitable location where you can quietly observe nature. This could be a park, a public garden, a tree-lined street, or even your own backyard or balcony, as long as you can see a good variety of natural elements such as trees, plants, and flowers.

### Step 2: Choose Your Time

Shadow and light can dramatically change throughout the day. You might want to pick a specific time to observe – sunrise, midday, and sunset can each offer a different palette of shadows and light. For a more comprehensive observation, you might even return at different times of the day.

**Step 3: Observe Mindfully**

Take a comfortable seat and begin to observe the interplay of light and shadow around you. Notice how the light filters through the leaves, creating patterns on the ground. Look at the shadows cast by trees or flowers. Observe how the sunlight highlights certain aspects of the plants, trees, or flowers, bringing out their colours or textures.

**Step 4: Engage Your Senses**

As you observe, try to engage all your senses. Listen to the sounds of nature around you. Feel the warmth of the sun on your skin or the coolness of the shadows. Smell the fresh scent of the greenery or flowers. This will help to deepen your connection with the natural world.

**Step 5: Reflection**

After your observation session, take a few moments to reflect on your experience. What did you notice? What surprised you? How did the experience make you feel? Reflection is an integral part of this practice as it allows you to internalize your observations and heightens your awareness.

**Step 6: Regular Practice**

Make this practice a regular part of your routine. Over time, you might start noticing subtle changes with the changing seasons or weather, further enhancing your appreciation of nature's beauty and the passage of time.

The practice of observing shadow and light in nature can be a deeply grounding experience. It encourages a sense of presence, enhances perception, and cultivates an appreciation for the beauty and complexity of the natural world.

# Benefits

Engaging in shadow and light observations can bring numerous benefits to a person's mental health and well-being. This simple practice allows us to deepen our connection with nature and heighten our perception of its beauty and the passing of time.

One of the primary benefits of shadow and light observations is the opportunity to cultivate mindfulness and present-moment awareness. As we sit in a quiet spot, attentively observing how the shadow and light play on natural elements, we become fully immersed in the present experience. We notice the intricate patterns, the interplay of colours, and the ever-changing shapes. This focused awareness helps to quiet the mind, promote relaxation, and reduce stress and anxiety.

Engaging in shadow and light observations also encourages a sense of wonder and appreciation for the beauty of nature. We begin to notice the subtle nuances and details that we might have otherwise overlooked. The play of shadows and light adds depth and dimension to the natural elements, revealing their inherent beauty. This heightened perception can bring a sense of awe and inspiration, nurturing our emotional well-being and fostering a greater connection with the natural world.

Furthermore, shadow and light observations provide an opportunity for reflection and introspection. As we witness the passing of time through the shifting shadows and changing light, we are reminded of the transient nature of life. This reflection can bring a sense of perspective and help us appreciate the present moment. It allows us to connect with the rhythms of nature and find solace in the cyclical nature of existence.

In addition to the mental and emotional benefits, engaging in shadow and light observations also offers an opportunity for gentle physical activity and relaxation. Finding a comfortable spot to sit and observe encourages us to slow down, breathe deeply, and be present in our bodies. This mindful engagement with nature can promote a sense of grounding, tranquillity, and overall well-being.

In summary, shadow and light observations provide

numerous benefits to a person's mental health and well-being. By engaging in this practice, we can cultivate mindfulness, deepen our appreciation for nature's beauty, foster a sense of wonder, and find solace in the passage of time. It is a simple yet profound way to connect with the natural world and nourish our overall well-being.

*The play of shadow and light, cast by the mist, makes the tree in this photo I took appear mythical, as if it's walking.*

# Practice 23: Early Morning Strolls

Try to take walks early in the morning when the city is still quiet. It's a magical time when you can hear more birdsong and feel closer to nature. Early morning strolls can be a profoundly peaceful and grounding experience. Here's a step-by-step guide to help you get the most out of this practice.

## Instructions

### Step 1: Plan Your Route

Identify a route that will allow you to experience as much of nature as possible. This could be a local park, a tree-lined street, or even just a quieter part of your city where you can see the sky clearly. Try to find a route that is safe and where you will be undisturbed.

### Step 2: Set Your Alarm

Choose a time early in the morning, ideally around sunrise. This is often when the city is at its quietest, and you can hear the natural world waking up.

### Step 3: Dress Appropriately

Check the weather the night before and dress appropriately for your walk. You want to be comfortable and mindful of the changing temperatures that can occur in the early morning.

**Step 4: Start Your Walk**

Begin your walk in a calm and relaxed state. As you stroll, keep your pace slow and steady. This is not about exercise, but rather about connecting with nature and your surroundings.

**Step 5: Engage Your Senses**

Pay attention to your senses as you walk. Listen for birdsong, feel the cool morning air on your skin, smell the freshness of the morning, and watch the colours in the sky change as the sun begins to rise.

**Step 6: Practice Mindfulness**

Try to remain present during your walk. If your mind wanders to your to-do list or worries, gently bring your focus back to your senses and the nature around you.

**Step 7: Reflect and Gratitude**

Once you've finished your walk, spend a few minutes reflecting on your experience. What did you notice? How do you feel? This is also a good time to express gratitude for the opportunity to connect with nature and for the new day ahead.

Regular early morning strolls can become a meditative practice that not only connects us with nature, but also helps to clear our minds, set a positive tone for the day, and increase our overall well-being.

# Benefits

Embarking on early morning strolls can have profound benefits for a person's mental health and well-being. This magical time of day, when the city is still quiet and the world is just beginning to wake up, offers a unique opportunity to feel closer to nature and experience its tranquillity.

One of the primary benefits of early morning strolls is the sense of calm and peacefulness they provide. As you step outside and start your walk, you enter a world that is yet untouched by the bustling activity of the day. The quietude allows for a deeper connection with nature, as you can hear the gentle rustling of leaves, the soothing melodies of birdsong, and the hushed whispers of the wind. This serene environment fosters a sense of tranquility, allowing you to leave behind the stresses and worries of everyday life.

Engaging in early morning strolls also offers a chance

to practice mindfulness and be fully present in the moment. As you walk, focus your attention on your surroundings. Observe the subtle changes in lighting as the sun begins to rise, notice the different colours painting the sky, and appreciate the fresh and invigorating air. By immersing yourself in the present experience, you cultivate a state of mindfulness that helps calm the mind and reduce anxiety.

Additionally, early morning strolls provide an opportunity for gentle physical activity. The act of walking, especially in nature, promotes physical well-being and helps to invigorate the body. It stimulates blood flow, releases endorphins, and can contribute to improved mood and increased energy levels throughout the day.

Furthermore, these morning walks offer a chance for reflection and setting a positive tone for the day ahead. As you stroll along, take moments to reflect on your thoughts, feelings, and intentions. Use this time to cultivate gratitude for the beauty of nature and the gift of a new day. By consciously appreciating these blessings, you can foster a positive mindset and a sense of optimism.

In summary, early morning strolls provide numerous benefits to a person's mental health and well-being. They offer an opportunity to connect with nature, practice mindfulness, experience tranquillity, engage in gentle physical activity, and set a positive tone for the day. By incorporating this practice into your routine, you can enhance your overall well-being and start each day with a renewed sense of peace and gratitude.

# Practice 24: Rain Walks

Walking in the rain, properly dressed of course, can be a deeply immersive natural experience. It's also a great way to observe urban wildlife, as many animals and insects become more active after the rain. Walking in the rain can be a very refreshing and invigorating experience. Here are some steps to help you enjoy rain walks safely and mindfully.

# Instructions

**Step 1: Check the Weather Forecast**
Before planning a rain walk, make sure to check the weather forecast. Ensure that it's a regular rainfall, and there are no warnings of severe weather conditions like thunderstorms or heavy downpours.

**Step 2: Dress Appropriately**
Wear waterproof clothing, including a rain jacket or poncho, waterproof pants, and rain boots. You can also bring an umbrella for added protection, but try to use it sparingly to fully immerse in the experience.

### Step 3: Choose Your Route

Select a safe route for your walk. This could be a well-maintained path in a local park, a quiet street, or any open space with trees and greenery around. If possible, avoid areas with heavy traffic to minimise getting splashed by passing cars.

### Step 4: Begin Your Walk

Start your walk, keeping your pace slow and comfortable. The aim here isn't to reach a destination but to enjoy the journey. Feel the sensation of raindrops on your skin, and breathe in the unique smell of rain.

### Step 5: Engage Your Senses

Pay attention to the sound of the rain hitting different surfaces, observe the raindrops on leaves and puddles forming on the ground, touch the rain-soaked bark of a tree. Noticing these small details can create a profound connection with nature.

### Step 6: Notice Wildlife

Many animals, birds, and insects tend to be more active after rain. If you're lucky, you might see earthworms, snails, and other creatures. Observe them without disturbing their natural behaviour.

**Step 7: Reflect on the Experience**

After your walk, take a moment to reflect on the experience. How do you feel? What did you notice?

Remember, the goal of a rain walk is to connect with nature and your inner self. It's a perfect opportunity to practice mindfulness, be present in the moment, and appreciate the beauty of nature in its different forms.

# Benefits

Rain walks can offer a deeply immersive and rejuvenating experience, allowing you to connect with nature in a unique way. Properly dressed for the weather, walking in the rain can be a refreshing and invigorating practice that offers several benefits for your mental health and well-being.

One of the primary benefits of rain walks is the sensory experience they provide. As raindrops fall gently on your skin and create a soothing rhythm, you become fully present in the moment. The sound of rain hitting different surfaces, the smell of wet earth, and the touch of rain-soaked foliage engage your senses, creating a profound connection with the natural world. This sensory immersion can help calm the mind, reduce stress, and bring a sense of tranquillity.

Rain walks also offer a unique opportunity to observe urban wildlife. After the rain, many animals and insects become more active, taking advantage of the moisture and the abundance of food. As you walk, keep an eye out for birds seeking shelter, earthworms emerging from the soil, or snails gliding along wet surfaces. Observing these creatures in their natural habitat can evoke a sense of wonder and appreciation for the interconnectedness of all living beings.

Additionally, rain walks provide a chance to embrace a childlike sense of adventure and spontaneity. By stepping out into the rain, you are breaking away from the ordinary and embracing the beauty of the present moment. This sense of playfulness and letting go can help alleviate worries, shift perspectives, and foster a greater sense of joy and freedom.

Furthermore, rain walks can serve as a form of mindfulness practice. As you stroll through the rain, fully present and attuned to your surroundings, you cultivate a state of mindfulness. Each step becomes intentional, and your focus on the sensory experience of the rain helps anchor you in the present moment, allowing thoughts and worries to dissipate.

In summary, rain walks offer a range of benefits for your mental health and well-being. They provide a sensory and immersive experience, facilitate observation of urban wildlife, evoke a sense of playfulness and adventure, and foster mindfulness. By embracing rain walks, you can embrace the beauty of nature, nurture a deeper connection with yourself and the world around you, and find moments of joy and tranquillity even in the midst of a rainy day.

# Conclusion

# Beneath Our Feet, Above Our Heads: Unearthing Our Ancestral Wisdom for a Harmonious Future

I want to acknowledge that many of the practices I have offered you have been inspired to varying degrees by indigenous ways of knowing and being.

As such, as we reflect upon the ancient wisdom of indigenous cultures and the relevance it holds for modern society, it is crucial to acknowledge an often-overlooked fact: each of us, no matter where we come from or where we live, is ancestrally linked to indigenous cultures, or what I call our Earth Ancestors. This may seem a remote concept, but the truth of our genetic history reveals an undeniable lineage of our indigenous-earth ancestry. In each of us, echoes of ancient wisdom whisper tales of interconnectedness and harmony with nature.

As Chief Seattle noted, "Humankind has not woven the web of life. We are but one thread within it. Whatever we do to the web, we do to ourselves. All things are bound together. All things connect."

• • •

# Our Forgotten Connection: The Richness of Ancestral Wisdom

Consider the richness of my own Scottish heritage. In the depths of time, my ancestors followed pagan beliefs, viewing humanity and nature as one. Their spiritual connection with the land, mirrored in their rituals and folklore, illustrated a profound understanding of ecological balance and respect for all life forms. Stone circles and ancient trees served as sacred sites, illustrating an early recognition of the intrinsic value of the natural world. They celebrated the turning of the seasons, marking the cycles of life and the interplay between human society and the Earth. This deep-rooted philosophy mirrors that of many indigenous cultures worldwide, a testament to the universal ancestral wisdom we share.

. . .

# The Seduction of Modern Life: Ignoring Our Historical Notes

Yet, in the midst of technological advancement and the fast pace of modern life, this ancestral connection is often forgotten. The stories our DNA carries - tales of living in harmony with the Earth, of understanding the intricate web of life, of reciprocal relationships with nature - seem to have faded into the background. It's not that these stories have disappeared; rather, we have become adept at overlooking them, seduced by the allure of material wealth and disconnection from the natural world.

. . .

# Our Inherent Capacity: The Essence of Indigenous Wisdom

Yet, these historical notes encoded in our very being continue to resonate with the essence of indigenous wisdom. They bear testament to our inherent capacity for nurturing deep connections with nature and with each other. Uncovering this ancient knowledge can offer transformative insights into our current global predicaments. It serves as a potent reminder that the wisdom of living in harmony with nature is not alien to us; it's a fundamental part of who we are.

In essence, the principles of reciprocity, connection, interconnectedness, simplicity, community, and cooperation are not just the hallmarks of indigenous cultures; they are universal virtues embedded in our shared human heritage. In each of us lies the potential to reclaim and rekindle these ancestral connections, reminding us that we are, in fact, a part of nature, not apart from it.

As Luther Standing Bear, Oglala Lakota Chief, notes, "The old people came literally to love the soil, and they sat or reclined on the ground with a feeling of being close to a mothering power...The soil was soothing, strengthening, cleansing, and healing..."

. . .

# Coming Home: Rekindling Our Connection with Nature

Therein lies our shared challenge and opportunity: to reawaken these echoes of ancient wisdom within us and weave them into the fabric of our modern lives. As we draw from this wellspring of ancestral knowledge, we can envision and create a future that honours our interconnectedness with all life, fostering a world of balance, reciprocity, and enduring sustainability. In so doing, we come full circle, honouring our indigenous roots, rekindling the wisdom of our ancestors, and awakening the potential for a harmonious future. It is a journey of remembering, a journey of becoming, a journey home.

. . .

# Tapping into the Timeless Wisdom: The Akashic Records and Ancestral Lifeways

In conclusion, I would like us to consider another perspective that offers a unique and compelling viewpoint on our relationship with our ancestry: the concept of the Akashic Records. Predominantly featured in theosophical and anthroposophical doctrines, the Akashic Records are believed to be a universal repository of all human experiences, thoughts, and actions that have occurred in the past, present, or future. It's like a cosmic library that captures the essence of every human journey, including our own and those of our ancestors.

The Law of Conservation of Energy, a widely accepted scientific principle, states that energy cannot be created or destroyed, only transformed or transferred from one form to another. Connecting these concepts then, one might suggest that the energy of our thoughts, words, and actions doesn't just dissipate; it's encoded in the etheric plane, contributing to the Akashic records.

Suppose we consider energy as information (as it's often referred to in the field of quantum physics). In that case, our collective experiences, encoded as energy, are never lost but instead transformed and stored in this metaphysical database. This idea proposes a form of immortality and interconnectedness, implying that not only our actions but our ancestors ripple through time and space, impacting the cosmos in ways we may not fully comprehend. It can be a compelling concept to consider, especially when thinking about our responsibility towards future generations and the legacy we leave behind.

Even as we acknowledge that our modern lifestyles are distinct from our ancestral lifeways, the concept of the Akashic Records suggests that the knowledge and wisdom of our forebears still exist within us all. They are not lost but exist in a different plane, waiting for us to tap into them. Even as the world around us changes, these records are believed to hold steady, preserving the essence of human experience across time and space.

Accessing these records requires a profound shift in our consciousness, a kind of mental and spiritual reorientation. It requires us to move beyond the confines of linear time and material reality, opening our minds to the existence of a metaphysical realm that holds the imprints of all human experiences. While this concept might seem abstract or even esoteric, it serves as a potent metaphor for our inherent ability to connect with our ancestral wisdom.

If we allow ourselves to embrace this perspective, we might find that the wisdom of our ancestors is not as distant as it seems. By opening ourselves to the possibility of the Akashic Records, we essentially acknowledge that the wisdom of our ancestors continues to exist and can still guide us. We affirm that we carry within us the echo of their experiences and their understanding of the world.

In essence, the Akashic Records, much like the concept of epigenetic memory and the collective unconscious, highlight that our disconnection from our ancestral wisdom is not an insurmountable barrier. It is a veil that we have drawn over our own perception. By reorienting our focus and striving to reconnect with our ancestral heritage, we can pull back this veil, rediscover the wisdom of our forebears, and imbue our modern lives with their timeless insights.

In conclusion, in our quest for a sustainable future, this reconnection may prove more vital than ever. By tapping into the wisdom preserved in the Akashic Records, we can remind ourselves of our deep-seated ties with nature, recognise the value of reciprocity and respect for the Earth, and bring forth a worldview that can help us navigate the challenges of our times. As we tread this path of reconnection, we come to understand that our roots run deep, and the wisdom of our ancestors is not just our heritage - it's our guiding light towards a harmonious and prosperous future.

# About The Author

Dr. Rodney King, is an Ecopsychologist and Mindful-Leadership Expert residing on the beautiful Isle of Man. His life's work orbits around the central theme of 'Rediscovering Our Roots,' where he explores the rich intersections of Nature's Intelligence, Ancestral Knowing, and Primal Skills Mastery. His unique approach guides individuals to delve into the heart of nature's wisdom, unlocking the keys to personal development and leadership effectiveness. He helps his clients align their life rhythms with those of the natural world, creating a harmonious balance that fosters personal growth and an innate sense of well-being.

Through his articles on his blog, coaching and guiding work, he provides insights into the profound influence of natural cycles on our lives and underscores the importance of understanding and embodying these patterns to enhance our daily experiences and interactions. In addition to his practice, Rodney actively contributes his insights to various platforms, inspiring thousands to forge deeper connections with nature and themselves. His captivating writing and transformational teachings can be accessed through his website, www.naturelead.earth.

Always drawn to the call of the wild, Rodney continues to unravel nature's mysteries, translating them into practical wisdom for modern living and leadership.

# References

1. Thoreau, H. D. (1862). *Walking*. Atlantic Monthly.
2. Macey, D., & Brown, M. (1998). *The Dictionary of Cultural Literacy*. Houghton Mifflin.
3. Williams, R. (2007). *Culture and Society, 1780–1950*. Columbia University Press.
4. Dunlap, R. E., & Catton, W. R. (1994). Struggling with Human Exemptionalism: The Condition of Sociology. *The American Sociologist*, 25(1), 5-30.
5. Naess, A. (1984). A Defence of the Deep Ecology Movement. *Environmental Ethics*, 6(3), 265-270.
6. Hickel, J. (2021). *Less Is More: How Degrowth Will Save The World*. Random House.
7. Fowers, B. J. (2005). Virtue and psychology: Pursuing excellence in ordinary practices. *American Psychological Association*.
8. Pink, S. (2018). *The Future is Now: An Optimistic View of Society*. Viking Press.
9. Jackson, T. (2009). *Prosperity without growth: Economics for a finite planet*. Earthscan.
10. Wilkinson, R., & Pickett, K. (2010). *The spirit level: Why greater equality makes societies stronger*. Bloomsbury Press.
11. Forbes, J. D. (1978). *Columbus and Other Cannibals: The Wetiko Disease of Exploitation, Imperialism, and Terrorism*. Seven Stories Press
12. Levy, P. (2013). *Dispelling Wetiko: Breaking the Curse of Evil*. North Atlantic Books.
13. Festinger, L. (1957). *A Theory of Cognitive Dissonance*. Stanford University Press.
14. Durning, A. T. (1992). *How much is enough? The consumer society and the future of the Earth*. W. W. Norton & Company.
15. Buzzell, L., & Chalquist, C. (2009). *Ecotherapy: Healing with Nature in Mind*. Sierra Club Books.
16. Louv, R. (2008). *Last Child in the Woods: Saving Our Children from Nature-Deficit Disorder*. Algonquin Books.
17. Roszak, T., Gomes, M. E., & Kanner, A. D. (Eds.). (1995). *Ecopsychology: Restoring the Earth, Healing the Mind*. Sierra Club Books.

18. Lent, J. (2022). *The web of meaning: Integrating science and traditional wisdom to find our place in the universe.* Profile Books Limited.
19. Dawkins, R. (1976). *The Selfish Gene.* Oxford University Press.
20. Tomasello, M. (2014). *A Natural History of Human Thinking.* Harvard University Press.
21. Maddison, A. (2007). *Contours of the world economy 1-2030 AD: Essays in macro-economic history.* Oxford University Press.
22. Piketty, T. (2013). *Capital in the twenty-first century.* Belknap Press.
23. Jasanoff, S. (2015). Future imperfect: science, technology, and the imaginations of modernity. *In Dreamscapes of Modernity: Sociotechnical Imaginaries and the Fabrication of Power.* University of Chicago Press.
24. Crist, E. (2013). On the poverty of our nomenclature. *Environmental Humanities, 3*(1), 129-147.
25. Berger, P. L., & Luckmann, T. (1966). *The social construction of reality: A treatise in the sociology of knowledge.* New York: Anchor Books.
26. World Economic Forum. (2022). *Global urbanization and material consumption.* Retrieved from https://www.weforum.org/agenda/2022/04/global-urbanization-material-consumption/
27. Kelly, R. L. (2013). *The lifeways of hunter-gatherers: The foraging spectrum.* Cambridge, UK: Cambridge University Press.
28. Diamond, J. (1997). *Guns, germs, and steel: The fates of human societies.* New York, NY: Norton.
29. White, L. (1967). The historical roots of our ecologic crisis. *Science, 155*(3767), 1203-1207.
30. Keller, D.R., & Golley, F.B. (2000). *The Philosophy of Ecology: From Science To Synthesis.* University of Georgia Press.
31. Passmore, J. (1974). *Man's responsibility for nature: Ecological problems and Western traditions.* New York, NY: Scribner.
32. Merchant, C. (1980). *The death of nature: Women, ecology, and the scientific revolution.* San Francisco, CA: Harper & Row.

33. Cohen, J. (2011). Science and humanities in the age of enviro-mentalism: The end of nature and the post-natural condition. *Green Letters*, 15(1), 37-55.

34. Ponting, C. (2007). *A new green history of the world: The environment and the collapse of great civilizations*. New York, NY: Penguin.

35. Moore, J. W. (2015). *Capitalism in the web of life: Ecology and the accumulation of capital*. Verso Books.

36. Steffen, W., Rockström, J., Richardson, K., Lenton, T. M., Folke, C., Liverman, D., & Schellnhuber, H. J. (2019). Trajectories of the Earth System in the Anthropocene. *Proceedings of the National Academy of Sciences*, 115(33), 8252-8259.

37. Wenner, M. (2020). Human Exceptionalism. In T. K. Shackelford & V. Zeigler-Hill (Eds.), *Encyclopedia of Personality and Individual Differences* (pp. 1-4). Springer.

38. Finlay, L. (2021). Human Exceptionalism and the Imago Dei: A Response to Recent Criticisms. *Themelios*, 46(1), 142-159.

39. Bastian, B., Costello, K., Loughnan, S., & Hodson, G. (2012). When closing the human–animal divide expands moral concern: The importance of framing. *Social Psychological and Personality Science*, 3(4), 421–429.

40. *Holy Bible: New International Version*. (2011). Grand Rapids, MI: Zondervan.

41. Sorabji, R. (1993). *Animal Minds and Human Morals: The Origins of the Western Debate*. Cornell University Press.

42. Benzoni, F. (2006). *The Human Imprint on the Environment: The Beginning of the Anthropocene Epoch?*. Enciclopedia Italiana.

43. Hatfield, G. (1992). Descartes on animals. *The Philosophical Quarterly*, 42(167), 219-227.

44. Malm, A. (2015). *Fossil Capital: The Rise of Steam-Power and the Roots of Global Warming*. Verso.

45. Leopold, A. (1949). *A Sand County Almanac and Sketches Here and There*. Oxford University Press.

46. Klein, N. (2014). *This Changes Everything: Capitalism vs. the Climate*. Simon & Schuster.

47. Nisbet, E. K., & Sachs, N. J. (2016). Nature Relatedness and Emotional Wellbeing. In G. Fleury-Bahi, E. Pol, & O. Navarro (Eds.), *Handbook of Environmental Psychology and Quality of Life Research* (pp. 231-247). Springer.

48. Abram, D. (1996). *The Spell of the Sensuous: Perception and Language in a More-than-Human World*. Vintage.
49. Capra, F. (1996). *The Web of Life: A New Scientific Understanding of Living Systems*. Anchor Books.
50. de Waal, F. (2016). *Are We Smart Enough to Know How Smart Animals Are?* W. W. Norton & Company.
51. Cajete, G. (2000). *Native Science: Natural Laws of Interdependence*. Clear Light Publishers.
52. Capra, F., & Luisi, P. L. (2014). *The Systems View of Life: A Unifying Vision*. Cambridge University Press.
53. Merchant, C. (2006). *The scientific revolution and the death of nature*. Isis, 97(3), 513-533.
54. Bacon, F., & et al. (2013). *The New Organon*. Cambridge University Press.
55. Descartes, R. (1637). *Discourse on the Method*.
56. Hobbes, T. (1651). *Leviathan*.
57. Soble, A. (1998). *Pornography, Sex, and Feminism*. Prometheus Books.
58. Locke, J. (1690). *Two Treatises of Government*. Cambridge University Press.
59. Smith, A. (1776). *An Inquiry into the Nature and Causes of the Wealth of Nations*. W. Strahan and T. Cadell.
60. Marx, K. (1867). *Capital, Volume I*. Verlag von Otto Meisner.
61. Hidaka, B. H. (2012). Depression as a Disease of Modernity: Explanations for Increasing Prevalence. *Journal of Affective Disorders*, 140(3), 205–214.
62. Doran, P., & Kinchin, I. (2019). *Re-thinking Economics: Exploring the work of Pierre Bourdieu*. Routledge.
63. Hakemy, L. (2017). The rise of capitalism: what it means for the environment. *University of Toronto Quarterly*, 86(4), 147-163.
64. Marshall, G. (2015). *Don't Even Think About It: Why Our Brains Are Wired to Ignore Climate Change*. Bloomsbury USA
65. Crutzen, P. J. (2006). The "Anthropocene". In *Earth System Science in the Anthropocene* (pp. 13–18). Springer.
66. Lewis, S. L., & Maslin, M. A. (2015). Defining the Anthropocene. *Nature*, 519(7542), 171–180.
67. Aikenhead, G. S., & Ogawa, M. (2007). Indigenous knowledge and science revisited. *Cultural Studies of Science Education*, 2(3), 539–620.

68. United Nations, Department of Economic and Social Affairs, Population Division (2018). *The World's Cities in 2018*—Data Booklet (ST/ESA/SER.A/417).
69. Hartig, T., Mitchell, R., de Vries, S., & Frumkin, H. (2014). Nature and Health. *Annual Review of Public Health, 35*, 207-228.
70. Steffen, W., Broadgate, W., Deutsch, L., Gaffney, O., & Ludwig, C. (2015). The trajectory of the Anthropocene: The Great Acceleration. *The Anthropocene Review*, 2(1), 81-98.
71. Lindeberg, S. (2010). *Food and Western Disease: Health and Nutrition from an Evolutionary Perspective*. Wiley-Blackwell.
72. Eaton, S. B., Konner, M., & Shostak, M. (1988). Stone agers in the fast lane: Chronic degenerative diseases in evolutionary perspective. *American Journal of Medicine*, 84(4), 739-749.
73. United Nations (2018). *68% of the world population projected to live in urban areas by 2050, says UN*. United Nations Department of Economic and Social Affairs.
74. Gluckman, P. D., Hanson, M. A., & Beedle, A. S. (2007). Early life events and their consequences for later disease: A life history and evolutionary perspective. *American Journal of Human Biology*, 19(1), 1-19.
75. Hoogland, C. T., & Ploeger, A. (2022). Evolutionary psychopathology and the mismatch hypothesis. *In Evolutionary Psychopathology* (pp. 25-50). Springer, Cham.
76. Bratman, G. N., Hamilton, J. P., & Daily, G. C. (2012). The impacts of nature experience on human cognitive function and mental health. *Annals of the New York Academy of Sciences*, 1249(1), 118–136.
77. Eaton, S. B., Konner, M., & Shostak, M. (1988). Stone agers in the fast lane: Chronic degenerative diseases in evolutionary perspective. *American Journal of Medicine*, 84(4), 739-749.
78. Lindeberg, S. (2010). Food and Western Disease: Health and Nutrition from an Evolutionary Perspective. Wiley-Blackwell.
79. Li, N. P., van Vugt, M., & Colarelli, S. M. (2017). The Evolutionary Mismatch Hypothesis: Implications for Psychological Science. Current Directions in Psychological Science, 27(1), 38-44.

80. Hoogland, C. T., & Ploeger, A. (2022). Evolutionary psychopathology and the mismatch hypothesis. *In Evolutionary Psychopathology* (pp. 25-50). Springer, Cham.
81. Little Bear, L. (2000). Jagged worldviews colliding. In M. Battiste (Ed.), *Reclaiming indigenous voice and vision* (pp. 77-85). UBC Press.
82. Zylstra, M. J., Knight, A. T., Esler, K. J., & Le Grange, L. L. (2014). Connectedness as a core conservation concern: An interdisciplinary review of theory and a call for practice. *Springer Science Reviews*, 2(1-2), 119-143.
83. Ives, C. D., Abson, D. J., von Wehrden, H., Dorninger, C., Klaniecki, K., & Fischer, J. (2018). Reconnecting with nature for sustainability. *Sustainability Science*, 13(5), 1389-1397.
84. Lehman, B. (2019). Returning to nature: How reconnection with the natural world can improve individual well-being and global health. *Environmental Justice*, 12(3), 84-89
85. Kimmerer, R. W. (2013). *Braiding sweetgrass: Indigenous wisdom, scientific knowledge, and the teachings of plants.* Milkweed Editions.
86. Basso, K. H. (1996). *Wisdom sits in places: Landscape and language among the Western Apache.* University of New Mexico Press.
87. Gifford, R. (2014). Environmental psychology matters. *Annual Review of Psychology*, 65, 541-579.
88. Zylstra, M. J., Knight, A. T., Esler, K. J., & Le Grange, L. L. (2014). Connectedness as a Core Conservation Concern: An Interdisciplinary Review of Theory and a Call for Practice. *Springer Science Reviews*, 2(1-2), 119-143.
89. Capaldi, C. A., Dopko, R. L., & Zelenski, J. M. (2014). The relationship between nature connectedness and happiness: a meta-analysis. *Frontiers in Psychology*, 5, 976.
90. Cacioppo, J. T., & Patrick, W. (2008). Loneliness: *Human nature and the need for social connection.* W. W. Norton & Company.
91. Fiske, S. T., Cuddy, A. J., Glick, P., & Xu, J. (2002). A model of (often mixed) stereotype content: competence and warmth respectively follow from perceived status and competition. *Journal of personality and social psychology*, 82(6), 878–902.

92. Steffen, W., Richardson, K., Rockstrom, J., Cornell, S. E., Fetzer, I., Bennett, E. M., & Sörlin, S. (2015). Planetary boundaries: Guiding human development on a changing planet. *Science, 347*(6223).

93. Yazzie, R. (1996). "Navajo Philosophy of Learning and Pedagogy." In J. Reyhner (Ed.), *Teaching Indigenous Languages* (pp. 59-66). Northern Arizona University.

94. Townsend, M., & McWhirter, B. (2005). Connectedness: A review of the literature with implications for counseling, assessment, and research. *Journal of Counseling & Development, 83*(2), 191-201.

95. Ferrari, A. J., Charlson, F. J., Norman, R. E., Patten, S. B., Freedman, G., Murray, C. J. L., ... & Whiteford, H. A. (2013). Burden of depressive disorders by country, sex, age, and year: findings from the global burden of disease study 2010. *PLoS medicine*, 10(11).

96. Samele, C., Fazzi, L., & Charlton, J. (2022). The Mental Health Foundation's 2018 UK study of stress: are we coping?. *Journal of Public Mental Health, 21*(2), 100-112.

97. Dezutter, J., Luyckx, K., & Wachholtz, A. (2013). Meaning in life in chronic pain patients over time: associations with pain experience and psychological well-being. *Journal of Behavioral Medicine, 36*(2), 200-210.

98. Tavella, G., & Parker, G. B. (2020). Is the 'biophilia hypothesis' still relevant? Reviewing the impact of disconnection from nature on depressive mood. *Australian & New Zealand Journal of Psychiatry, 54*(3), 225-235.

99. Burls, A. (2007). People and green spaces: Promoting public health and mental well-being through ecotherapy. *Journal of Public Mental Health, 6*(3), 24-39.

100. Fretwell, L., & Greig, M. (2019). 'Ecotherapy – a forgotten ecosystem service: A review'. *Public health, 172*, 137-142.

101. Frances, K., Nadkarni, N. M., & Burls, A. (2021). The Positive Impact of Nature on Human Health and Well-being: Applications to Elderly Populations. *Frontiers in Psychology, 12*.

102. Ivtzan, I., Chan, C. P., Gardner, H. E., & Prashar, K. (2013). Linking religion and spirituality with psychological well-being: Examining self-actualisation,

meaning in life, and personal growth initiative. *Journal of Religion and Health, 52*(3), 915-929.

103. Kaplan, S. (1995). The restorative benefits of nature: Toward an integrative framework. *Journal of Environmental Psychology, 15*(3), 169-182.

104. Kaplan, S. (2001). Meditation, restoration, and the management of mental fatigue. Environment and Behavior, 33(4), 480-506.

105. Frantz, C. M., Mayer, F. S., Norton, C., & Rock, M. (2005). There is no "I" in nature: The influence of self-awareness on connectedness to nature. Journal of Environmental Psychology, 25(4), 427-436.

106. Farkić, J., & Taylor, E. (2019). From the treadmill to the wild: Reflections on the embodied experience of being (in) nature. *Sport, Ethics and Philosophy, 13*(3), 216-229.

107. Hanley, A. W., Garland, E. L., & Black, D. S. (2020). Use of mindful awareness to foster self-care during nature-based mindfulness practice. *Mindfulness, 11*(1), 113-122.

108. Franco, L. S., Shanahan, D. F., & Fuller, R. A. (2017). A review of the benefits of nature experiences: More than meets the eye. *International Journal of Environmental Research and Public Health, 14*(8), 864.

109. Andrews, M. (2018). Reconnecting with nature: The therapeutic benefits of sensory experience in the outdoors. *Clinical Psychology Forum, 316*, 28-32.

110. Lengieza, M. L., & Swim, J. K. (2021). Engaging with nature increases nature connectedness and pro-environmental behavior. *Journal of Environmental Psychology, 75*, 101550.

111. Plotkin, B. (2008). *Nature and the human soul: Cultivating wholeness and community in a fragmented world.* New World Library.

112. Snell, T. L., & Simmonds, J. G. (2012). Spirituality in the work of Theodore Roszak: Implications for contemporary ecopsychology. *European Journal of Ecopsychology, 3*, 41-54.

113. Ballew, M. T., & Omoto, A. M. (2018). Absorption: How nature experiences promote awe and other positive emotions. *Ecopsychology, 10*(1), 26-35.

114. Rogers, N., & Bragg, E. A. (2012). The power of participation: Environmental education and ecological

stewardship. *Journal of Environmental Education*, 43(4), 211-224.

115. Taylor, P. (2012). An ecological approach to educational research: Where's the post in eco?. *Environmental Education Research*, 18(2), 188-206.

116. Scott, D., Brinkhurst, M., & Bridgeland, J. (2014). Walking, the first steps in the transition to a more sustainable lifestyle. *Human Ecology Review*, 20(2), 81-93.

117. Reinders, H. S. (2017). More than mere nature: Awe and the sublime in two contemporary nature films. *Journal of Religion, Film, and Media*, 3(2), 49-68.

118. Smith, J. A., Flowers, P., & Larkin, M. (2009). *Interpretative Phenomenological Analysis: Theory, Method and Research*. London: Sage Publications Ltd.

119. Peavy, G. M., Salmon, D. P., Jacobson, M. W., Hervey, A., Gamst, A. C., Wolfson, T., Patterson, T. L., Goldman, S., Mills, P. J., & Khandrika, S. (2009). Effects of Chronic Stress on Memory Decline in Cognitively Normal and Mildly Impaired Older Adults. *American Journal of Psychiatry*, 166(12), 1384–1391.

120. Yuen, H. K., Lee, T. M. C., & Hogan, W. (2012). The Role of Physical Exercise in Regulating Pheomelanin and Eumelanin Synthesis in Hair Bulb Melanocytes. *Journal of Exercise Science & Fitness*, 10(1), 27–35.

121. Perini, R., Brehm, J. M., Unützer, J., & Stensland, M. (2019). The Impact of Physical and Mental Health on Life Satisfaction: Evidence from the Patient Health Questionnaire (PHQ-9) and the Short Form Health Survey (SF-12) for Older Americans. *Age and Ageing*, 48(4), 517-523.

122. Bratman, G. N., Hamilton, J. P., & Daily, G. C. (2012). The Impacts of Nature Experience on Human Cognitive Function and Mental Health. *Annals of the New York Academy of Sciences*, 1249(1), 118–136.

123. Kaplan, R., & Kaplan, S. (1989). *The Experience of Nature: A Psychological Perspective*. Cambridge University Press.

124. Berman, M. G., Kross, E., Krpan, K. M., Askren, M. K., Burson, A., Deldin, P. J., Kaplan, S., Sherdell, L., Gotlib, I. H., & Jonides, J. (2012). Interacting with Nature Improves Cognition and Affect for Individuals with Depression. *Journal of Affective Disorders*, 140(3), 300-305.

125. Olivos, P., & Clayton, S. (2016). Self, Nature and Well-being: Sense of Connectedness and Environmental Identity for Quality of Life. In G. Fleury-Bahi, E. Pol, & O. Navarro (Eds.), *Handbook of Environmental Psychology and Quality of Life Research* (pp. 107-126). Springer.

126. Richardson, M., McEwan, K., Maratos, F., & Sheffield, D. (2019). Joy and Calm: How an Evolutionary Functional Model of Affect Regulation Informs Positive Emotions in Nature. *Evolutionary Psychological Science,* 5(4), 308–320.

127. Houlden, V., Weich, S., de Albuquerque, J. P., Jarvis, S., & Rees, K. (2018). The Relationship Between Greenspace and the Mental Wellbeing of Adults: A Systematic Review. *PLoS ONE,* 13(9).

128. Rosenberg, E. L. (2017). Mindfulness and consumerism. *In Handbook of Consumer Psychology.* Taylor & Francis Group.

129. Kabat-Zinn, J. (2003). Mindfulness-based interventions in context: Past, present, and future. *Clinical Psychology: Science and Practice,* 10(2), 144-156.

130. Langer, E. J. (2000). Mindful learning. *Current Directions in Psychological Science,* 9(6), 220-223.

131. Hanley, A. W., Nakamura, Y., & Garland, E. L. (2017). The Mindfulness-to-Meaning Theory: Extensions, Applications, and Challenges at the Attention–Appraisal–Emotion Interface. *Psychological Inquiry,* 28(4), 232-248.

132. Brown, K. W., & Ryan, R. M. (2003). The benefits of being present: Mindfulness and its role in psychological well-being. *Journal of personality and social psychology,* 84(4), 822-848.

133. MacKerron, G., & Mourato, S. (2013). Happiness is greater in natural environments. *Global Environmental Change,* 23(5), 992-1000.

134. Nisbet, E. K., Zelenski, J. M., & Murphy, S. A. (2022). The Nature Relatedness Scale: Linking individuals' connection with nature to environmental concern and behavior. *Environment and Behavior,* 41(5), 715-740.

135. Bringslimark, T., Hartig, T., & Patil, G. G. (2009). The psychological benefits of indoor plants: A critical review of the experimental literature. *Journal of Environmental Psychology,* 29(4), 422-433.

136. Amel, E. L., Manning, C. M., & Scott, B. A. (2017). Mindfulness and sustainable behavior: Pondering attention and awareness as means for increasing green behavior. *Ecopsychology*, 9(1), 14-25.
137. Mason, O., & Brady, F. (2020). The Psychotomimetic Effects of Short-Term Sensory Deprivation. *Journal of Nervous and Mental Disease*, 196(10), 783-785.
138. Jirásek, I. (2013). Spirituality and health among adolescents and young adults in the Czech Republic: A psychometric analysis of the Daily Spiritual Experience Scale. *Health Education Journal*, 72(4), 469–476.
139. Lumber, R., Richardson, M., & Sheffield, D. (2017). Beyond knowing nature: Contact, emotion, compassion, meaning, and beauty are pathways to nature connection. *PLOS ONE*, 12(5)
140. Kellert, S. R., Heerwagen, J., & Mador, M. (2017). *Biophilic design: the theory, science, and practice of bringing buildings to life*. John Wiley & Sons.